# ENGENDERING VIOLENCE

# Engendering Violence

Heterosexual interpersonal violence
from childhood to adulthood

160101

MYRA J. HIRD
*Queen's University, Belfast*

# Ashgate

Published by
Ashgate Publishing Limited
Gower House
Croft Road
Aldershot
Hampshire GU11 3HR
England

Ashgate Publishing Company
131 Main Street
Burlington, VT 05401-5600 USA

Ashgate website: http://www.ashgate.com

**British Library Cataloguing in Publication Data**
Hird, Myra J.
    Engendering violence : heterosexual interpersonal violence
    from childhood to adulthood
    1. Violence  2. Heterosexuals  3. Interpersonal conflict
    I. Title
    305.3

**Library of Congress Control Number:**  2001099949

ISBN 0 7546 0916 2

Printed and bound in Great Britain by Antony Rowe Ltd, Chippenham, Wiltshire

# Contents

# Acknowledgements

Several people have supported me, in many different ways, during the writing of this book. I thank Kimberly Abshoff, Maureen Baker, Tarani Chandola, Nigel Clark, Chris Davies, Sylvia Easton, Liz Frazer, Jenz Germon, Paula Gunn, Zubaida Haque, Judy Haschenburger, Janet Hird, Roger Hood, Sue Jackson, Stevi Jackson, Allison Kirkman, Jane Kubke, Jason Mabbett, Henrietta Moore, Mike Noble, Terry O'Neill, Anna Paris, George Pavlich, Sasha Roseneil, Chris Rovee, Liz Stanley, Reece Walters and Lynda Williams.

I also thank Katherine Hodkinson for her kind encouragement and support during the publishing process.

I dedicate this book to my parents, Barbara and Brian Hird, and to my best friend Anth Krivan.

Chapter 1

# Mapping the Discourses of Heterosexual Interpersonal Violence

## Personal Safety and Public Discourses of Gender Difference

Messages about personal safety, from the protection of property to dating protocol, pervade our everyday lives. These messages usually offer advice about protecting ourselves from strangers. Women, in particular, are expected to prevent their own victimization by avoiding certain places, walking in the company of others, predicting when people's tempers are getting out of hand and generally monitoring danger. Men's lives, on the other hand, are not as restricted.[1] Indeed, men often accompany women home at night because it is assumed that men protect women from harm. Boys, also, do not typically learn the same number of personal safety strategies as girls and are also allowed to go out at night more often and to more places than girls. Yet the most likely victims of assaults by strangers are young men.[2]

From a sociological perspective, public discourses about personal safety are interesting because they contradict how males and females actually experience violence in their daily lives. An apparently gender-neutral discourse reflects, in fact, the experience of heterosexual masculinity and a particular understanding of danger, harm and violence. This is the reason that personal safety discourse remains largely silent about females' most likely assailants: male acquaintances, male friends, male parents, male siblings, boyfriends and male spouses.[3] The following narrative inquires into the subject of heterosexual interpersonal violence. This analysis takes as its starting point the contradiction between personal safety discourses and women's and men's experiences of interpersonal violence, which by far accounts for the majority of society's everyday violence. In this analysis I will extend an existing critical discourse reassessing how, theoretically and empirically, gender and heterosexual interpersonal violence intersect.

In contemplating this map, I initially want to draw attention to three signposts on the interpersonal violence landscape: gender, space and relationship. First, contrary to movies such as *Fatal Attraction* and *Disclosure*, most violence (whether intimate or stranger-to-stranger) is committed by males. This does not mean that males as a group condone violence. It is to say that statistics consistently reveal that men commit the majority of physical and sexual assaults, and homicides. Men are also responsible for the majority of violence towards women. In the United States, the assault of women by their (ex)partners is the second highest form of serious injury after male to male assault. Interpersonal violence against women has reached such epidemic proportions in the United States that Surgeon General Everett Koop proclaimed domestic violence to be the number one health problem for American women (Schenck, 1992). The National Clearinghouse of the Defense of Battered Women estimates an incidence of domestic assault is reported every fifteen seconds in the United States (Spaid, 1993) and some researchers in the area of wife assault have coined the phrase 'a marriage license is a hitting license' (Gelles and Straus, 1988). More than a million women in the United States seek medical attention each year for injuries sustained from (ex)husbands, (ex)partners and (ex)lovers. Surgeon General Antonia Novella claims that domestic violence causes more injuries to women than the collective injuries sustained from rapes, muggings and car accidents (Spaid, 1993). Yet the Federal Bureau of Investigation reports that wife battering is the most underreported crime in America (Wenzel, 1993).

Second, contrary to everyday assumptions, males are more likely to be assaulted in public whilst females are more vulnerable to violence in their own homes. For example, statistics for England and Wales show that men are more likely to be victims of assault outdoors and women are most likely to be attacked in their own homes or the home of their attacker (Government Statistical Service, 1994). In Canada in 1994, approximately forty-nine percent of homicides, sixty-one percent of sexual assaults and forty-nine percent of physical assaults occurred in private residences (Statistics Canada, 1995). Most murders (fifty-seven percent) in Australia in 1995 also took place in private dwellings. Assault is the largest category of offenses against the person in Australia and they most frequently occurred in private dwellings. In 1995 New Zealand (1996) statistics recorded that approximately fifty-two percent of indecent assaults, seventy-seven percent of coercive sexual relations and sixty percent of sexual violation occurred within the home.

Finally, the relationship between perpetrator and victim is also important. Data from the United States, the United Kingdom, Canada, Australia and New Zealand all confirm that heterosexual interpersonal violence, whether homicide, sexual assault or physical assault, is largely committed by persons known to the victim. Moreover, most offenses are committed in circumstances of interpersonal conflict.

## Emergent Themes

### Gender and Difference

This book coincides with a major theoretical shift in gender and interpersonal violence theories. Coming to terms with the complexities of patriarchy, gender relations, sexuality, subjectivity, colonialism and globalization has prompted a challenge to traditional conceptualizations of the relationship between gender and interpersonal violence. This past decade in particular has produced a proliferation of theories on subjectivity and gender relations, work taken up by a number of feminist scholars (see Flax, 1987; Butler, 1990; Haraway 1990; Hooks, 1990; Nicholson, 1990; Yeatman, 1990; Fraser and Nicholson, 1994). More recently, under the rubric of 'new sociology of gender theories' (Dobash, Dobash and Noaks, 1995), a combination of feminist, poststructural and postmodern theory is attempting to deconstruct these concepts by calling attention to their essentialist girding.[4] Poststructural and postmodern theories of gender radically call into question the notion of a pre-social (sexed) body, arguing instead that bodies are configured through social, political and cultural discourses. These theories posit an historical and changeable body, on which all possible configurations of power and signification are inscribed.

Because postmodern theories posit a post-socially sexed body (that sexual difference is created rather than emerges from some innate origin), these theorists are concerned to theorize *how* we understand gender and the mechanisms through which gender is reproduced (cf. French, 1985; Sydie, 1987; Spelman, 1988; Butler, 1990; Rhode, 1990; Lorber, 1994). They suggest that the 'essence' of meaning is no more than the very establishment and maintenance of binary opposites. Thus, we can only know what 'man' is through its *opposition*, 'woman'. The female is everything that is absent from the male and *vice versa*. Gender difference is sustained through a play of absence and presence 'revealing that what appears to be outside a given system is always already fully inside it; that which seems to be natural is historical' (Namaste, 1996: 196). Postmodern works call attention to sociological discussions of 'women' and 'men' predicated on this essentialist binary opposition. Emerging theories of gender argue that gender identity is assembled, fragmentary and shifting and that individuals 'practice' gender through a variety of mechanisms (Rose, 1996).

An increasing body of scholarship has begun to challenge this bi-polar construction of gender and the *a priori* association between violence and masculinity. These works argue that many studies reify rather than challenge the association between masculinity and violence. Bi-polar configurations of gender and the *a priori* association of violence with masculinity fail to acknowledge the wide variation in female and male behavior. By framing males as violent and females as passive, the complexity of human behavior is vastly over-simplified. Specifically, the variety of violent behavior *within* each gender is ignored whilst differences *between* genders are exaggerated (Hyde, 1990). The link between masculinity and violence is tautological: violence occurs in society because males are violent and males are violent because they are males. Moreover, an exclusive focus on male violence denies females' reality such that violent women are silenced. Violent women are defined as deviant, undermining women's status as fully responsible human beings (White and Kowalski, 1994). This effectively maintains male power as 'men prefer not to dwell on women's aggression because it (is) an ugly sign of potential resistance' (Campbell, 1993: 143). It is the problematic association between gender and violence that poststructural and postmodern theorists seek to challenge by exploring the social conditions under which we have come to associate violence with masculinity, and the ways in which our current understanding of violence reinforces gender divisions.

The attribution of particular characteristics to women and men remains one of the most common practices in society. Zygmut Bauman (1997) explores how 'strangers' are created by society as a means of bringing order to an unstable, shifting environment. Bauman attempts to understand human atrocities such as the holocaust as an outcome of the creation of strangers and the implied threat that strangers make to the established order. To discriminate against large numbers of people on the basis of race, ethnicity, religion and social class requires a discourse which positions a 'them' as representative of everything to which 'we' stand opposed. Discrimination becomes possible and manageable when those being discriminated against are so different from us as to be not really fully human. This creation of strangers may also be applied to gender, as society's insistence on the creation and maintenance of differences between women and men serves to impose order onto social relations. Indeed, gender difference is one of the most enduring binaries in our language: we position ourselves against the 'opposite' sex. This positioning, as this book will argue, provides a key element in understanding the persistence of heterosexual interpersonal violence in society.

*Power and Investment*

Public discourses identify apparently stable gender identities at the local, social, and group levels (Connell, 1995). These gender identities are arranged within a power-knowledge nexus in which gender identities are hierarchically ordered. It is on these masculinities and femininities which recent analyses of heterosexual interpersonal violence focus. Gendered performances ('Baywatch babe', 'computer geek', 'dyke') identify certain combinations of actions and objects through which gender is practiced.[5] Certain masculinities, and a minority of femininities, are assembled around the practice of violence. The macho homophobic male 'gay basher', for instance, is only able to identify himself as 'straight' by articulating his difference from gay men.

If we understand individuals to take up or perform particular subject positions, Hollway's (1984) notion of 'investment' provides a useful conceptual tool for connecting the agency involved in this performance and violence as action.[6] Investment refers to a combination of emotional commitment and vested interest in terms of perceived rewards. It is here that the link between subject positions and power is made explicit because subject positions are positioned in relation to others and take on meaning only in that relation (Moore, 1994). The choice of subject positions is both limited and bounded by historical-structural institutions and each individual's agency is expressed in the choice from this limited set of subject positions. This is not to say that all subject positions are equal and that individuals are 'free' to pick and choose between them. Quite the contrary: some subject positions clearly carry greater social rewards than others, particularly with respect to race, sexuality, ethnicity, age and so on.

Recent analyses further consider interpersonal violence to be an active expression of power relations between individuals. When individuals act violently, they often explain (read 'justify') their actions in terms of a reaction to an unfulfilled need as in 'my wife didn't have my dinner ready on time so I hit her'. This man's violence is based on a particular conceptualization of individuals, relationships and social interaction. First, the statement made above would only be possible when social interaction is viewed in terms of the exchange of commodities (Kappeler, 1995). This idea is by no means novel in the context of most relationships in society: my relationship with my bank teller, grocery store cashier and so on are all based on the exchange of commodities (exchanging money for goods). However, we do not typically make these terms of exchange explicit. A key element in the 'trade in relationships' is power. The man does not want his wife to make his dinner on time because he is forcing her to; she is to make his dinner willingly. In getting his dinner served on time, what this man really achieves is the capturing of his wife's will. Of course this annihilates the intended meaning of social interaction which is the free giving of things (feelings, care and so on) as gifts. In our social relationships, we do not want the goods and services from our family, partner and friends. We want their subjectivities embodied in those goods and services. Thus social interaction involving violence silences subjectivity. The Gramscian (1971) notion of power proves useful as it is formulated less on physical force and more on a sustained relation of 'voluntary' submission. Moreover, whilst the will (intent) of the individual is crucial to the definition of violence, the response of the person being demanded also needs addressing. When the man demands that his wife provide dinner on time, her doing this (which we tend to interpret as failing to resist violence) does not erase the violence of his demand. Nor does her resisting (throwing the dinner in this face, walking out the door) define his demand as violent. In other words, it is not the response to violence that defines violence, it is the will and the action of the person seeking need fulfilment that defines what constitutes violence (Frye, 1983). The conceptualization of heterosexual interpersonal relationships as a site of commodity exchange and the concomitant public discourse in which personal relationships are anything *but* an exchange, helps us to understand the structural context in which interpersonal violence takes place.

**Aims of the Book**

This book aims to explore these emerging themes in the heterosexual interpersonal violence literature. First, it seeks to explore those discourses which create and maintain *gender differences*. Socio-biology, psychology and sociology largely inform everyday understandings of gender. It will then proceed to examine how children learn to identify gender as a major symbolic marker used to differentiate individuals and order the social environment. Children must learn to *perform* the particular gender to which they have been assigned and to see themselves as *opposite* to the 'other' gender. I will argue that learning to organize our social worlds using bi-polar symbols configured as oppositional creates *strangers*. Once we begin to think of certain groups of individuals as our opposite, as strangers, we lay the foundational girding necessary for the justification of violence.

The book's major theme concerns the link between gender and violence, and in particular the performance of masculinity. To further explore this link necessitates the examination of a crucial aspect of hegemonic masculinity: heteronormativity. Through an exploration of adolescent dating relations, I will argue that, at a societal level, social relations are structured around expectations of heteronormativity, which structure sexual relations between women and men as coercive. By linking discourses of gender differences and expectations regarding gender performance and heterosexual interpersonal relations, I want to be able to understand how and why interpersonal violence persists as one of the most common forms of violence in society.

The book will further explore the argument that heterosexual interpersonal violence may be understood as an outcome of the *investment* in performances predicated on the production of gender difference. The chapters which focus on adult heterosexual interpersonal violence will draw on the theories of interpersonal relations as commodity exchange briefly outlined here. To continue the example, the man who hits his wife 'because' she did not provide dinner on time conceptualizes the relationship with his wife in terms of the rightful fulfilment of his needs. Within this conceptualization, the husband must attempt to control her subjectivity in order that she give 'freely' those goods and services that he wants. Her subjectivity is directly bound up with his subjectivity. In reality, of course, this man has set himself an impossible task: no individual's subjectivity may be completely controlled. The best he can do is to get his wife to take up a subject position (caring, giving, suffering wife) that will not threaten his subject position (heterosexual, head-of-household, boss). He acts violently when he interprets that his subject position has been threatened. Thus violence, and the threat of violence, is not the sole domain of the heterosexual marital relationship: the threat to subject positions occurs in all personal relationships.

The potential of new theories of gender and interpersonal violence must also be advanced with a healthy dose of skepticism. Feminist theory involved in contemporary debates about gender deconstruction does so in the context of a backlash against feminism (Faludi, 1992). Moreover, there is a strong feeling amongst many 'front-line' feminists that we are in danger of losing gender altogether in our efforts to deconstruct 'woman' and replace it with 'multiple genders'. Feminism began with the explicit political project of liberating girls and women from the oppressions of patriarchy and many feminists wonder where this goal of liberation has gone. Many feminists note that this new emphasis on the meaninglessness of the category of 'woman' has come, significantly, at the same time that the voices of women of color are finally being heard (Hooks, 1990). There is a real danger that academic women involved in post-structuralist/postmodern debates about gender are expounding on a power located within patriarchy rather than against it. Cognizant of these dangers, I have nevertheless proceeded with an analysis of heterosexual interpersonal violence using recent theories of gender and power. I do this because I argue that women's agency is predicated on our acceptance as full human being; hence responsible and agentic. Moreover, I contend that attributing any particular characteristics to women (whether passivity or caring) does nothing to enfranchise women in the long run.

**Defining Concepts**

A genealogy of violence demonstrates that what society considers 'violent' is both historically and contextually dependent. Certainly, for instance, violence is not only considered destructive, but also productive and necessary, as the rhetoric produced during war attests. It is important to recognize this productive aspect of violence, which belies a complex moral signification which extends from the macro-level to individual interpersonal relationships.

Any sustained analysis of interpersonal violence must also recognize the presence of other signifiers including 'aggression', 'negotiation', 'argument', 'debate', 'conciliation' which are related in ambiguous and shifting ways to interpersonal violence.[7] Describing someone as 'violent' means that person has probably caused great physical harm to another person or animal. The use of force, in this context, is usually deemed excessive. However, this text will argue that whilst the term violence does signify extreme harm, it is also a key signifier of certain performances of masculinity. Thus violence is sometimes used as a 'short-hand' for masculinity.

Following most theoretical work on violence, I have chosen to separately define psychological, physical and sexual violence in order to lend a specificity to the discussion. However, I do not suggest that these types of violence occur (or usually) separately. Nor do I adhere to a hierarchy such that physical and sexual violence are assumed to be more harmful than psychological violence (Kelly, 1988). The following definitions assume an intention to harm and the interaction of at least two individuals as I want to emphasize the agency (or 'will') involved in violence as well as its relation to social interaction. Physical violence, in the following narrative, will consist of any physical act which intends to harm in some way. This includes pushing, shoving, grabbing, wrestling or pinning down, throwing an object at someone, scratching, biting, slapping, punching, hitting with an object, kicking, strangling and using a weapon such as a knife or gun. Sexual violence will include non-consenting sexual relations, unwanted sexual touching, or forcing an individual to engage in degrading sexual activity.[8] Psychological violence will include intimidating, terrorizing, humiliating, insulting, isolating the person from family and/or friends, yelling and/or screaming at an individual in order to induce fear, destroying the person's property or controlling the person's movements. I will return to these definitions in chapter four.

**Signposting the Narrative**

This book concerns heterosexual, same-age interpersonal violence. By focusing on these sets of relations I am not suggesting that violence does not take place in same-sex interpersonal relationships or between individuals of different age. Indeed, child abuse is well documented and an increasing literature concerns violence in gay and lesbian relationships.[9] I have chosen to particularly focus on same-age violence because it constitutes such a great percentage of societal violence. Added together, bullying, adolescent dating violence and spousal[10] violence constitute the majority of 'everyday' violence that individuals, and particularly females, experience. However, as this chapter has highlighted, the 'everyday' violence that the media tends to focus on is that violence perpetrated by strangers.

In undertaking this project, I have drawn on research from the United States, Canada, England, Australia and New Zealand. Employing data from these Western countries invites a recognition of similarities and differences in heterosexual interpersonal violence across cultures and societies. This focus also presents an immediate bias and one which I share with many Westerners. I have chosen these countries as they are the ones with which I am most familiar. This is not to say, far from it, that interpersonal violence does not take place outside these countries. Nor is it to say that the 'solution' to interpersonal violence will come from any of these countries.

I have organized the book as follows. Chapter Two reviews the dominant theoretical explanations of heterosexual interpersonal violence. The major focus of this chapter concerns an exploration of those discourses which invoke gender difference to explain interpersonal violence. Recent reformulations within poststructuralism and postmodernism challenge these discourses to re-consider understandings of gender, power and interpersonal relations. The next four chapters are concerned with heterosexual interpersonal violence at the three main stages of human development. Chapter Three focuses on child violence through an exploration of bullying, sexist behavior in the classroom and sibling violence. The major argument here is that childhood involves the learning of a complex system of signification, of which gender represents a prominent sign. Children learn to accent differences between genders at the same time as they minimize differences within genders. Aggressiveness is a key marker of masculinity, and male children in particular learn to use aggression and violence to signify their gender. By learning to understand their own gender, children are learning to identify themselves as part of a gender community which is posited in opposition to the 'other' gender. I will argue in this chapter that this configuration of 'us' and 'them' facilities the use of interpersonal violence. Chapter Four focuses on adolescent dating violence. Basing the analysis on my own recent research in the United Kingdom, this chapter argues that heteronormativity structures sexual relations between women and men as coercive, and that adolescents most often explain this coercion through recourse to socio-biological discourses of gender difference. Chapter Five concerns adult male violence, focusing on the context of heterosexual interpersonal relationships as the site of commodity exchange. I further the argument made in the previous chapter that heteronormativity provides a societal structure within which interpersonal violence takes place. The major aim of this chapter is to examine the investment that men make in particular masculinities which normalize violence. I will argue that when men use violence they can access a ready-to-hand discourse which normalizes their use of violence: that is hegemonic heterosexual masculinity. Chapter Six examines female adult interpersonal violence in order to challenge those discourses which posit an *a priori* association between masculinity and violence. Chapter Seven concludes the book by reviewing the main arguments presented and suggesting how new theories of gender may assist in understanding heterosexual interpersonal violence.

## Notes

1　According to the 1992 British Crime Survey, men reported feeling safe enough to walk the streets alone at night, whilst women reported not feeling safe to do the same.

2　It is usually heterosexual men who report feeling most safe from stranger violence. Gay men regularly experience psychological and physical violence (termed 'gay bashing') and, like women, incorporate a variety of personal safety strategies in their negotiation of public spaces.

3　We might viably explain this absence of female reality in public discourse on safety through a recognition of the significance attached to marriage and families as social institutions. Society relies on these institutions, and ideals of love and commitment that lead individuals into marriage and families, to reproduce children, provide consumer units and free labor. The importance attached to these institutions is reflected in the finding that even some individuals practicing 'alternative lifestyles' such as gays and lesbians are engaged in a political struggle to secure the right to marry and adopt children. As a society, we remain attached to ideas about love and the grouping of people into fairly isolated units, without a concomitant recognition that it is in this context that most girls and women experience violence. We would need to carefully re-consider our understanding of love and commitment to include violence in their definitions.

4　For the sake of convenience I use the words 'poststructural' and 'postmodern' interchangeably here. These terms are commonly interchanged, although they do have different histories and are used to different effects. Some argue that post-structuralism may be differentiated from postmodernism by the former's critique of modernism (Huyssen, 1984) and as such can not make the ontological and epistemological leap necessary to form post-modern analysis. This distinction begs the question of what postmodernism might offer, if anything, that may be differentiated from poststructural/modern approaches to subjectivity. No doubt this debate could be raged on other seas such as those of aesthetics, culture, economics, technology and globalization. If there are any differences, and there is by no means any consensus on this point, it perhaps stems from debate over contemporary conditions, their relation to the modern world and the centrality of difference to notions of subjectivity. Lyotard's (1984) abandonment of 'grand narratives' reflects a (post?)modern discomfort with claims to totalizing or universal theories of society. Whether sociology is, in fact, ready and willing to leave aside grand theories, there does appear to be a renewed interest in the politics of the subject. And whether we have concluded some world state called 'modern' and entered into a post-modern era is a question requiring a breadth and depth of discussion beyond the scope of this book. But more importantly, my concern to understand personal violence research renders this hypothesising less crucial. Rather than locate myself 'for' or 'against' postmodernism I invoke the term as a possible discourse in which to explore the problem. For further discussion see Smart (1990).

5    Whilst these categories are used both by researchers and public discourses, it is important to recognize the danger in using these categories, as they themselves become as fixed and rigid as binary notions of gender.

6    Subjectivity, on the other hand, necessarily means more than subject position, although these two terms are commonly conflated. Individuals practice a variety of subject positions dependent upon context, investment and biographical history and it is the opaque, fluid and unstable subjectivity of each individual that allows subject positions to be practiced.

7    In fact, the term 'violence' is much broader than the already ubiquitous term 'personal violence'. We speak of 'ideological violence', 'political violence', 'the violence of silence' and so on, all connotating, at least, some intention to, and effect of, harm.

8    I do not include here the consensual practice of sado-masochism.

9    For research on child abuse see Straus and Gelles (1980), Yllo and Bograd (1988). For research on lesbian battering see Lobel (1986), Renzetti (1992), Taylor and Chandler (1995).

10   Here I include non-marital relationships.

# Chapter 2

# Theoretical Challenges to the Study of Heterosexual Interpersonal Violence

Attempts to theorize heterosexual interpersonal violence most often originate from the disciplines of socio-biology, psychology and sociology. Popular media and everyday discourses with which we understand our experiences of interpersonal violence largely borrow from socio-biology and psychology. Although emanating from different theoretical standpoints, I want to argue that biological, psychological and sociological theories share a discourse predicated on the *a priori* association of masculinity with violence. That is, violence is positioned as a natural, immutable aspect of heterosexual masculinity. Given the concern to articulate an alternative way of conceptualizing the possible relationship between gender and heterosexual interpersonal violence, the major part of this chapter focuses on recent sociological analyses of gender, power and interpersonal relationships which challenge the immutable association between masculinity and violence.

## Socio-biological Explanations

Socio-biology provides one of the most pervasive, popular and enduring discourses on the relationship between gender and all forms of violence. At its most basic, this discourse is predicated on the assumption that aggression is inherent and natural to the human species. That is, certain genetically based and neurologically mediated variations in human beings predispose each gender toward certain behaviors. So, for instance, males are often described as having increased propensities for sensation-seeking and risk-taking, alcoholism, gambling and extreme extroversion. One of the most agreed upon variations has to do with aggressive 'instincts' which tend to be assigned to males, whilst females are categorized as more passive and nurturing. Contemporary socio-biological research on violence largely examines the influence of hormones and genes. Females, on average, have slightly lower levels of androgen and testosterone than males and this *slight average* difference has been linked to the different levels of aggression and violence found between the sexes.

Historically, the link between violence and gender was perhaps most famously argued through the theory of natural selection, developed by Charles Darwin in *The Origin of Species* (1859). The theory of evolution suggests that those physical and behavioral characteristics that increase the likelihood of survival in any species will come to predominate through a process of natural selection. Applied to interpersonal violence, this theory suggests that there may be some 'advantage' (in terms of survival) for males who use violence against females. Evolutionists note that, historically, females have devoted considerably more time and energy than males to caring for offspring. The theory suggests it is in females' maximum interest to choose male sexual partners who have certain advantageous characteristics (such as height, strength etc.) and it is in males' best interest to adopt strategies which will maximize the number of females with whom they will have sex (Wilson, 1975; Dawkins, 1989). Females supposedly evolve traits which maximize their efficiency in taking care of their offspring and males evolve traits which increase their chances of impregnating large numbers of females. It is not difficult to see how this theory has been employed to explain sexual coercion (see for example Ellis, 1989).

Similarly, in *On Aggression*, Konrad Lorenz (1966) described violence as a self-generating instinct occurring naturally in humans. Lorenz argued that violence increases in the individual until it is released by some external trigger.[1] Comparing human aggression with that of animals, Lorenz proposed that animals with physical characteristics designated for aggressive actions (such as claws and antlers) are also endowed with instinctual inhibitions against attacking members of its own species compared with humans who have no such physical characteristics.[2]

Despite the attractiveness of these simplistic arguments, biological theories make a number of problematic assumptions. Conceptualizing males as violent and females as passive masks the variety of violent behaviors found in society. Violence is not the sole domain of masculinity; nor is passivity exclusively feminine. Few biologists draw attention to data suggesting female violence is a significant problem. Biological theories also fail to explain why all men do not use violence. That males are almost exclusively motivated by a biological 'sex drive' is hopelessly reductive and can only be ascribed to male behavior in a *post-hoc* fashion (Cameron and Frazer, 1994). Moreover, Toner (1977) urges a great deal of caution when male sexual behavior is associated with an instinctual biological imperative. Ample anthropological evidence demonstrates that cultural attitudes and values equally determine the strength of the male 'sex drive' – indeed the term 'sex drive' is a cultural production in itself.

A sociological analysis argues that Western culture produces a discourse in which *social* differences between women and men are supposed to reflect *biological* differences. Biological explanations are used to describe differences in aggression, a wide variety of abilities, sexuality, sex and family life. Many books popularize the message that men and women are ultimately different and that this fundamental difference is self-evident. In an exposé of this approach to gender difference, Connell (1987) and others such as Williams (1995) argue that those practices which do not conform to evolutionary theory are termed 'biologically unhealthy' or 'evolutionary aberrations'. For Connell, socio-biology 'reflect(s) what is familiar back as science, and justif(ies) what many readers wish to believe' (1987: 69). That is, theories of biological determinism reflect back to the public, through a discourse of science, their familiar social arrangements in the making of difference:

> Men and women are, of course, different. But they are not as different as day and night, earth and sky, yin and yang, life and death. In fact, from the standpoint of nature, men and women are closer to each other than either is to anything else - for instance, mountains, kangaroos, or coconut palms. Far from being an expression of natural differences, exclusive gender identity is the suppression of natural similarities (Rubin, 1975, p.157).

As Rubin's remarks suggest, culture and social relations, in fact, amplify small differences in females and males to create differentially prescribed personality traits according to gender.[3]

Connell points out that one of the fallacies on which evolutionary theory, as applied to social phenomena, rests is that society is viewed as a system of open competition. Hormonal differences between males and females are used to suggest that males have a competitive advantage over females, so that in 'free competition' males will out-succeed females. Of course, an unbiased reading of history will demonstrate that there has never been a system of equal competition between females and males, or males and males for that matter. Another fallacy is that our culture's current social relations are the result of the human animal's pre-destination to reproduce. A wide variety of social arrangements would produce sufficient heterosexual intercourse to propagate the human species and provide enough child care to ensure children's survival. That advocates of biological determinism arrive at the nuclear family, bigamy or polygamy (any of which arrangement involves the female caring for young children and the male having at least one sexual partner) says more about the philosophy of the authors of this type of theory than it does about human social relations.

## Psychological Explanations

Psychological theories tend to focus on *a priori* factors (such as gender, social class, internal defense systems, the presence of mental illness and personality) considered to correlate with, or predict, heterosexual interpersonal violence. Empirical research tends to compare violent and non-violent individuals, seeking differences between these groups as possible explananda. Many people assume that interpersonal violence is positively correlated with social class, race, ethnicity, the consumption of alcohol/drugs, and is endemic to sub-cultures (read non-white) within which interpersonal violence is considered normal and acceptable. The presumed association between interpersonal violence and these descriptors arises from assumptions such as working-class people having less self-control, ethnic groups being misogynist and that alcohol/drugs cause violence. Many studies have attempted to establish a significant correlation between ethnicity, social class and interpersonal violence. Despite a continued presumption that these descriptors predict violence, no studies have found a consistently significant association between the ethnicity or race of either perpetrator or victim and interpersonal violence (O'Keeffe, Brockopp and Chew, 1986; Hird, 1995a, 1995b, 2000a). Similarly, no consistent relationship has been found between alcohol/drug use and interpersonal violence (Burcky, Reuterman and Kopsky, 1988; Stets and Henderson, 1991). It is possible, however, that using alcohol and/or drugs provides an excuse for males to initiate violence (Muehlenhard, 1988).

Many researchers have also investigated the 'transmission of violence' theory which suggests that violence, either experienced (as a victim), or witnessed (as in a father abusing the child's mother) will increase the likelihood that the individual will 'repeat' this violence in later life. Some evidence suggests that men who grew up in families in which their father assaulted their mother are more likely to assault their wives (Truscott, 1992). However, many men who abuse their wives did not grow up in violent homes. Moreover, the relationship between violence in the family of origin and women abused as adults has not been substantiated. Instead, practitioners tend to use knowledge of violence in the family of origin as a potential signal for violence during adulthood rather than assuming any direct causation.

Psychological theories also focus a great deal on personality factors hypothesized to be associated with interpersonal violence. With few exceptions, the personalities of the perpetrator and victim are measured in terms of how well they fit *a priori* notions of masculinity and femininity. There is often a conflation of personality factors and biological theory as aggression is assumed to be a male characteristic whilst passivity is 'naturally' feminine. For instance, Schultz (1960) described abusive husbands' behavior as the result of their rejecting mothers and wives who displayed 'masculine' characters.

Evaluating individuals' behavior according to how well they conform to pre-assigned gender characteristics inevitably leads female victims to be held accountable for male violence. For instance, Frude (1991) found that women who 'are highly critical, engage in frequent complaining, fight below the belt, use physical aggression themselves and behave in ways that...encourage jealousy' have a heightened risk of experiencing violence from their husbands. Gelles (1977) insists that women 'trigger [abuse through] nagging, criticizing, name-calling, and gibes about status or sexual performance'. Psychology draws on a notion of pathology to theorize violent men as mentally ill and their female victims as deriving masochistic gratification from the violence (West, Roy and Nichols, 1978). This pathology model is popular with the public. A recent survey found that mental illness was the most common reason individuals gave as to why some men rape women (Silver, 1991).

Perhaps the most significant problem with psychological theories of interpersonal violence is that, like biological theories, there is a necessary reliance on the invocation of gender difference. Differences between males and females are emphasized whilst differences within each sex are minimized. These essentialist gestures elaborate mechanisms through which small, average biological differences between females and males (themselves devoid of any intrinsic meaning) transform into large differentially prescribed personality traits. Psychological theories appear to uncritically accept statistics showing that males are more violent and create theories to explain *post-hoc* these findings. When confronted with findings of male passivity and female violence, psychological theories have little choice but to find these individuals 'deviant' to a norm created from this binary concept of gender (this will be illustrated in Chapters Five and Six). But many violent men demonstrate no psychological disturbance. And no consistent psychological patterns have been found for the minority of violent men who do evidence psychological disturbance. Attempts to provide a personality profile of victims reveals more about the effects of violence rather than anything about personality traits that 'precipitate' violence. Nevertheless, psychological theories often invest gendered personality traits with a 'truth' about violence. As Naffin writes:

> The characteristics developed in men which are said to reflect and to be 'expressive' of their gender role concerns, those of toughness, independence and aggression, according to these theories, have a tendency to conduce to criminality. In some versions of the theory, it is those males who become preoccupied with proving their masculinity, who become 'compulsively' masculine, who are especially prone to engage in crime. The traits encouraged traditionally in women are said to have the opposite effect. The womanly virtues of passivity and dependence encourage conformity. In those few women who deviate, these same traits condition the mode and the motive of offending (1985, p.365).

The effect of ascribing differentiated personality traits to males and females *a priori* is to ignore or re-interpret any indications of gender 'transgressions'. The violent acts of women are re-constructed such that women become 'deviant' or victims of men's violence. Balthazar and Cook (1984), for instance, explain the increase in female delinquency as more girls becoming 'masculine'. Non-aggressive men are similarly discursively re-constructed to become 'sissies' or 'poofters'. The corollary of this biological determinism is that both men and women's violent behavior is exonerated, increasing the likelihood that violent behavior will continue (Smart, 1976).

## Sociological Explanations

Because psychological theories tend to accept that particular characteristics are gendered, even the most critical studies can do no more than refine the relation between these characteristics and gender. In order to deconstruct the assumptions on which the attribution of gendered characteristics are made in the first place, we must turn to sociological theories.

A number of competing sociological theories have also attempted to explain heterosexual interpersonal violence. Popular theories have included functionalist theory, which argues that violence serves particular 'functions', both individually and at a societal level. Sub-cultural theory suggests that subcultures (such as the gangs of Los Angeles) form as a response to the dominant middle class, white culture. According to this theory, these subcultures maintain norms of aggressive masculinity and female passivity and condone male violence against females. Systems theory most often focuses on 'family violence' (Straus, 1973). Families are seen as a system reliant on the inter-functioning of each part. Family violence is analyzed in terms of the complex interaction of the system's parts rather than the result of individual pathology.

But arguably the most significant influence on sociological theories of heterosexual interpersonal violence is feminist theory. Indeed, to a large extent sociologists studying heterosexual interpersonal violence construct explanations dependent upon, or as a response to, feminist theory. Prior to feminist theorizing, interpersonal violence was scarcely discussed. What theorizing did exist suggested that interpersonal violence was uncommon, abnormal, endemic only to certain sub-groups such as the working-class, and the product of dysfunctional families. Feminists, working as researchers and practitioners, challenged these assumptions to articulate an entirely new way of seeing interpersonal violence within society.

## Re-thinking Gender

Feminist theories of the 1960s and 1970s highlighted gender as the major, or indeed single, determinant of interpersonal violence. Gender was removed from its positioning as *a* descriptor to *the* salient causal factor. Feminists argued that all individual relationships, families, social groups and institutions are structured and re-structured by gender. Violence against females was seen as transhistorical and transcultural, evident in all social classes, ethnic, racial and age groups.[4] This work was instrumental in changing the perception that wife assault was an infrequent phenomenon, practiced only by a minority of working-class, non-white men (Dobash and Dobash, 1979). These studies used feminist methods to voice the narratives of battered women themselves as well as those of experts on interpersonal violence.[5]

At this time, feminist scholarship depended upon the invocation of 'patriarchy', an umbrella under which all forms of violence against females could be understood and challenged politically. Patriarchy, in this context, designated the social, political, economic and cultural context in which women were both institutionally and individually subordinated by men. This focus extended to the economic subordination of women in terms of unequal treatment in the paid and unpaid work environment (Barrett, 1988). Marriage and the nuclear family were analyzed as sites of isolation and labor division (Schechter, 1982; Breines and Gordon, 1983). Central to this theorizing on interpersonal violence was the conceptualization of power as the most effective, last line-of-defense for patriarchy. Within patriarchy, all males potentially use power as a means of controlling females. Males, as a social group, benefit from female dependence, unequal treatment in the paid and unpaid work force and more subtly through the dividends of unequal power. In short, all males benefit from patriarchy: through the violence of some males towards some females, all males keep females in a state of fear (Brownmiller, 1975). Understood in these terms, violence does not represent a breakdown in society. Rather, male aggression and violence against females signifies the maintenance of a social order based on male privilege and power (Dworkin, 1987).

This early feminist work has since been critiqued for its over-emphasis of super-structural, monolithic forces supposed to 'cause' interpersonal violence. Moreover, a large proportion of early feminist theories of violence depended on a notion of patriarchy that emphasized *differences* between females and males and *the biological nature of these differences*. The sheer prevalence of interpersonal violence across diverse societies tempted the recourse to biology: boys and men are violent because of their hormones, genetics or the (multi-purpose and elusive) 'male drive'. However, this provided little insight into how or why some males act aggressively or violently whilst others do not. Nor did such a monolithic theory of patriarchy account for female violence in its own right. Whilst many feminist theories of violence carefully avoided any direct links between biology and interpersonal violence, the bulky apparatus of patriarchy invited this association.

Since second-wave feminism began to theorize the relationship between gender and violence, the theoretical landscape has changed considerably. From virtually nothing written on the subject of women and few women authors within academia, feminist works have exploded onto the academic scene. Coming to terms with the complexity of patriarchy, gender relations, sexuality, subjectivity, colonialism and globalization has resulted in a great deal of re-thinking in feminist scholarship. The 1990's, in particular, has seen a movement by some feminist scholars away from the consciousness-raising ethos of earlier feminism to much more theoretically rigorous research. What arguably began as a forced self-reflection from non-white, non-middle class, non-western women has moved into a proliferation of theoretical work on subjectivity and gender relations.

A number of feminists (for example, Flax, 1987; Butler, 1990; Haraway, 1990; Hooks, 1990; Nicholson, 1990; Yeatman, 1990; and Fraser and Nicholson, 1994) have taken on the task of articulating a highly theoretical body of knowledge on subjectivity and gender relations (McNeil, 1993). A combination of feminist, poststructural and postmodern thinking has recently produced what is called 'new sociology of gender' theories (Dobash, Dobash and Noaks, 1995). These theories mainly seek to re-conceptualize gender, power and violence. Traditionally, gender has referred to 'feminine' and 'masculine' characteristics. In these new theories, gender is not seen as a term relating to two units: male and female. Rather, gender is completely practiced, with as many variations as there are human beings.[6] According to these recent formulations, there is nothing inherent or 'natural' in the ascription of certain human qualities to males and other human qualities to females. In terms of theorizing interpersonal violence, discussion of 'men' and 'women' as homogenous categories has produced a great deal of frustration. The conviction that all men have power over women is articulated in feminist adages such as 'all men are potential rapists'. These statements do not tend to enjoy particular public popularity. Most of us know situations in which certain men do not have as much 'power' as women. Many individuals, male and female, have also experienced female aggression and violence. Similarly, many girls and women have trouble seeing themselves as 'victims'. Power has turned out to be much more elusive, intangible and nebulous than we thought. Newer theories are struggling to elaborate a theory of gender and violence using a more complex understanding of power.

Recent literature from the sociology of gender has moved towards 'multiple gender' theory. As a central scholar involved in this project, Connell (1987) re-theorized masculinity as an umbrella term signifying a structured set of hierarchical social relations amongst men founded on the subordination of women.[7] At the apex is the notion of hegemonic masculinity, dependent upon complex historically and context dependent inter-relations between social class, race, ethnicity, age, nationalism and so on. Subordinated masculinities and femininities are not only identified by relations of power 'but also in relation to a division of labor and patterns of emotional attachment, psychological differentiation and also institutional differentiation as part of collective practices' (Newburn and Stanko, 1994: 3). Connell's work was able to develop a more nuanced and reflective account of gendered social relations which recognizes differences *within* gender as well as *between* genders.

Contemporaneously, Connell's multiple gender theory invokes a particular notion of identity, as composed of a number of 'parts', often termed 'subject positions'. This conceptualization continues a fermented theoretical tendency towards a self composed of homogenous units. Nietzsche spoke of 'a multiplicity of subjects, whose interaction and

struggle is the basis of our thought and our consciousness in general'
(1968: 490). Likewise, George Herbert Mead and John Stuart Mill spoke of
'selves' and multiple 'me's' (Mill, 1987: 452; Mead, 1962: 142-44).
However, questions remain concerning the composition of subject positions
as well as their relation to the 'self': a conceptualization of the individual as
made up of parts risks implying a relative stability and fixidity to these
parts. In attempting to understand such a nebulous concept as identity, then,
preference has been afforded to the ways in which various identifiers fit
together, sometimes at the expense of differences *within* descriptors and
how such differences might shape experience. That is, the theoretical and
empirical strategy within sociology has been to retain a somewhat unified
notion of self. As Mullin (1995) has argued, analyses of subjectivity have
tended towards assimilation (privileging one 'part' and silencing others),
compartmentalization (keeping 'parts' separate) or indifference.

Broadly, then, we have seen a shift within sociology from the notion
of a unitary self to an assembled self (in the form of subject positions).
Postmodern theories extend this trend and reject all notions of a self, as
such, and focus instead on gender as performative. When anthropologists
have stressed the need 'to sift the sensationalized accounts of exotic
cultures for the real gold: the common features of humankind' (Gordon,
1991: 116), postmodern theory argues that the only possibly common
feature to be gleaned is performativity. As such, gender is more a product
or effect of discursive and material performance. Gender becomes a
chimera, a shifting assemblage that necessarily carries the possibility of
change. Individuals 'practice' gender through a large number of
mechanisms including comportment (how to walk, how to sit down, how to
bend over), artifacts (makeup, soccer uniform, high heels, workman's
boots), spaces (bedroom, doctors waiting room, toilet, restaurant, locker-
room), and objects (children's toys, gun, briefcase, car). Postmodern theory
suggests individuals are involved in a constant process of negotiating
contexts with the various interpretations that culture offers in any given
moment. Or, as Rose (1996) argues, women and men are subject to regimes
of practice through which they 'agent-ize' themselves as humans. Thus,
performativity emphasizes the possibility of change and transformation.

Central to postmodern analyses of gender is the deconstruction of
discourses on gender to reveal the extent to which such discourses are
imbued with polarity. As Simone deBeauvoir argued in her classic account:

> he is the subject, he is the Absolute – she is the Other. The category of the
> Other is as primordial as consciousness itself. In the most primitive societies,
> in the most ancient mythologies, one finds the expression of a duality – that
> of the Self and the Other (1953, p.16).

DeBeauvoir refers to a system of reference, of making sense of the world, dependent upon the identifying of a unitary and undifferentiated self through the identification of the other. It is through this system of bifurcation that the meaning of gender itself is established. We can only know what 'man' is through its *opposition*, 'woman'; the female is everything that is absent from the male and vice versa.

This idea is furthered by Derrida's (1976) notion of *supplementarity*, which refers to the 'essence' of meaning as the establishment and maintenance of a set of differences.[8] Thus, we can only know what 'man' is through its opposition, 'woman'. The female is everything that is absent from the male and vice versa. Difference is sustained through a play of absence and presence and 'reveals that what appears to be outside a given system is always already fully inside it; that which seems to be natural is historical' (Namaste, 1996: 196). Analyses now seek to deconstruct those discussions of 'women' and 'men' which are predicated on an essentialist binary opposition. Instead, gender identity is emphasized as an assemblage, both fragmentary and shifting.

## Re-thinking Power

Early feminist theories of interpersonal violence relied on the dominant conceptualization of power formulated in the 1960s and 1970s. Power was depicted as a zero-sum game in which one individual's possession of power necessarily meant his or her 'opponent's' lack of power. Power was seen as both monolithic and intransigent. Patriarchy signified the super-structural embodiment of power that maintained a system in which men have power *over* women. As MacKinnon argued 'gender is...a question of power, specifically of male supremacy and female subordination' (1987: 40). Violence and power became conflated, violence being the extreme, physical *expression* of power. This analysis of power often *ended* with the association of masculinity with violence, as in Brownmiller's famous dictum 'rape...is a conscious process of intimidation by which all men keep all women in a state of fear' (1975: 15).

In *Discipline and Punish*, Foucault (1979) formulates an entirely different conceptualization of power. Foucault presents power not as a substance that individuals either have or do not have, but as diffuse and subtle, circulating within and around social relations. Rather than a possession, power is a strategy; the ways in which 'maneuvers, tactics, techniques (and) functionings' are transmitted by and through individuals (Smart, 1985: 77). As such, there is really no such thing as power *per se*, only the bearing of multiple *local* mechanisms. Unlike early feminist formulations in which male power was conceived as both universal and wholly negative (the power of men to subordinate women), Foucault introduced the contingency of context and the insistence that power is productive. That is, all relationships are relationships of power; any form of collectivity requires relations of power which *produce* social beings. This is a power formulated less on physical force and more on a sustained relation of 'voluntary' subjectification (Gramsci, 1971).

The power that Foucault presents in *Discipline and Punish* suggests that power, in itself, has the capacity to completely discipline and regulate individuals. However, in his later work 'The subject and power' (1982), Foucault underscores the idea that power can only 'work' through free individuals. Power presupposes agency and 'although power is an omnipresent dimension in human relations, power in a society is never a fixed and closed regime, but rather an endless and open strategic game' (Gordon, 1991). Thus Foucault crucially distinguishes between power and violence. Whilst power may be practiced through agentic individuals, violence implies a complete lack of agency. The implications of this re-formulation include the need to re-visit our understanding of interpersonal violence. If it is power which defines gendered relations, this necessarily implies the possibility of resistance and subversion.

In terms of gender, our modern condition of self-knowledge necessitates that women and men both comprehend and accept bifurcated characteristics (O'Neill and Hird, 2001). Precisely because gender is neither immutable nor static, women and men are obliged to constantly reflect upon gender practice. Gender, like all other symbols involved with identity, must be interpreted and, even on a superficial level, this interpretation requires a social actor. As Brittan expresses, 'men are not simply the passive embodiments of the masculine ideology' (1989: 68). Thus particular power-knowledge nexus produces the 'truth' about gender: gender and power are wholly co-implicated.

This conceptualization begs a different set of questions concerned with the social conditions under which we have come to associate violence with masculinity, and the ways in which our current understanding of violence reinforces gender division. If aggression and violence have less to do with gender and more to do with power, then should not the central analytical move from the exploration of who is more violent to the analysis of the cultural, political and economic contexts which empower some males and females to act violently? In this new setting, we find theorizing on modern configurations of interpersonal relationships provide insights into the context in which interpersonal violence occurs.[9]

In creating a theory of multiple gender we do not simply want to replace the 'deviant' male with 'hegemonic masculine identity', thereby sustaining the assumption that violence is endemic to masculinity. A paradigm equating violence and masculinity has had the effect of producing research that conceptualizes male violence as 'normal' whilst rendering acts of female violence deviant.

These essentialist gestures elaborate mechanisms through which small biological differences between females and males (themselves devoid of any intrinsic meaning) transform into large differentially prescribed personality traits to remain unspecified. These gendered personality traits are invested with a 'truth' about violence. The effect of ascribing differentiated personality traits to males and females *a priori* is to ignore or re-interpret any indications of gender 'transgressions'. The violent acts of women are re-constructed so that she becomes 'deviant' or a victim of men's violence.

It is here that recent work within feminist criminology proves useful in attempts to evacuate *a priori* associations between gender and interpersonal violence. Feminist criminology has simultaneously achieved a focus on women's criminality in its own right as well as a critique of the discourse produced from this standpoint epistemology. If, at first, feminist theory seemed reluctant to embrace findings of female interpersonal violence, this has been more recently eclipsed by work within feminist criminology. That feminist criminology has historically sustained its focus on male oppression of women is hardly surprising given both the prevalence and seriousness of wife assault and its historical relegation as a matter of domestic rather than criminal concern. However, the often subtle omission of female violence has been found, as a consequence, in several such analyses.

In Chapter Six I will argue that new research on lesbian battering as well as increased concern with *a priori* conceptualizations of women as victims necessitates a re-thinking of assumptions concerning the role of gender in interpersonal violence. Kappeler (1995) asserts that feminist analyses of power and the discourse applied to women's oppression and men's dominance tend to be applied both wholly and individually. That is, individual men and women, and their behaviors towards each other, are defined *by their gender*. So women are, by definition, victims and men are perpetrators. We do not look past this equation because gender identity identifies and defines the actors' relationships. Kappeler (1995: 115) argues that through a process of 'discursive reconstruction' we accommodate instances of female desire for power, control and their behaviors of manipulation into a paradigm of female victimization and selflessness.

The ways in which violence is discussed as gendered is worth laboring. Critical criminology suggests that female violence is often ignored, trivialized or otherwise rendered harmless (see Allen, 1987; Kappeler, 1995; Naffin, 1985; Smart, 1995). Male violence, in contrast, receives attention, often in the form of tolerance (as in 'boys will be boys') or outright acceptance. Indeed, it is clear that society expects a certain degree of aggression and violence from males as this behavior is an intricate part of male gender performance. On the other hand, when women commit acts of interpersonal violence, society is faced with behavior that is in direct contravention to valued gendered social scripts. The reaction is often to consider the act of violence to be the product of mental disturbance: the violent woman becomes the *victim* of forces beyond her control (just as men are often considered to be the 'victims' of sexual drives beyond their control).[10] The consequences of making women passive non-agents is to further silence female volition and gender stasis through the bolstering of differentiation. Even in cases in which women are convicted of serial murders, these women are often relegated to the role of accomplice to the male (often a boyfriend or husband) who is seen as the real agent of the violent acts.

With these recent formulations of gender and power in mind, I now turn to the literature on childhood, adolescent and adulthood heterosexual interpersonal violence. I aim to illustrate that research does not support a monolithic attribution of a complex action such as interpersonal violence to the single determiner of gender. These chapters will attempt to argue that the creation and maintenance of gender *difference* helps sustain a set of social relations which produce the structure in which violence has become endemic to heterosexual interpersonal relationships. I want to effect a critical interpretation of research on heterosexual interpersonal violence from a position in which power relations do not cause this violence (Walzer, 1987). In other words, I will apply postmodern re-formulations of power, subjectivity and social relations to the study of interpersonal violence.

## Notes

1    In applications of evolutionary theory to violence against females, the female often seems to be this 'external trigger'. See, for example Snell, Rosenwald and Robey (1964); Gelles and Straus (1988).

2     Lorenz notes that the development of war machines has resulted in the high prevalence of violence in society because we have no internal inhibitions to using violence, as animals have.

3     Psychological tests have been widely criticized for their assumption that certain traits are more characteristic of one sex than the other. Beyond the inherent problems with statistical testing in which results that do not fit the theory can be easily discarded, there is the fundamental problem of how psychologists 'know' that the scales measure femininity and masculinity. Why scales posit males and females on opposite ends of the spectrum instead of, say, separate scales on which any individual could score highly on both scales, has more to do with the ideological assumptions underpinning the scales than it has to do with what is feminine and what is masculine.

4     Feminist empirical research has investigated diverse practices such as footbinding, infibrilation and gang rape to call attention to the fact that these practices are performed on girls and women *because they are female* (Daly, 1978).

5     Useful discussions of the development of feminist epistemology appear in Robert, (1981), Harding (1987), McCarl Nielsen (1990), Stanley (1990), Alcoff and Potter, (1993), Stanley and Wise (1993).

6     The notion that gender is practiced is taken up by Judith Butler who states:

> gender proves to be performative—that is, constituting the identity it is purported to be. In this sense, gender is always a doing, though not a doing by a subject who might be said to pre-exist the deed' (1990, p.24-25).

7     Others (such as O'Neill and Hird, 2001) refer to masculinities as located on a continuum with the dominant construct at one extreme and its antithesis, the effeminate homosexual, at the other.

8     Derrida is certainly not alone in exploring the establishment of meaning through difference. See also Irigaray (1985a, 1985b); Kirby (1997); Braidotti, (1989); Butler (1993); and Cornell (1992).

9     Michel Foucault, in a similar vein to his philosophical predecessor Frederick Neitzsche, was interested in exploring not so much those aspects of humanity that seemed to come under systems of reason (science, psychiatry, law etc.) but those aspects which defied such discourses. Whilst Neitzsche called into question the very definitions of good and evil, Foucault seems to have understood some 'essence' of humanity that might be revealed in the pursuit of 'limit-experiences': intoxication, sado-masochistic practices etc. In the paintings of Goya, waiting for Godot, the barbaric act of Pierre Riviere and even the historian and philosopher might voice this usually silent 'essence' of humanity consisting of a combination of 'impulses' which constitute the full continuum of desire and pleasure; it is 'the most internal, and at the same time the most savagely free of forces' (Foucault, 1965). This force is no shallow hastily erected murmur of testosterone levels. Foucault, like others before and since, alludes to an internal essence of destruction and sadism in humanity which is our very nature and is, indeed, as natural as any desires and pleasures. Where does this 'essence' come from? 'Everything that morality, everything that a botched society, has stifled in man (sic)...' (Foucault, 1965).

10    See Allen (1987) for a critical analysis of the ways in which the criminal justice system working in conjunction with the psychiatric discipline discursively maneuver the violent woman into a position of passivity.

# Chapter 3

# Learning the Difference that Gender Makes

Childhood involves learning a complex series of physical skills and social relations.[1] Children are required to assimilate a tremendous amount of information concerning social interaction and actively use this information to negotiate family, friends and school relations. Children are born into a system in which their gender has already been assigned, and learn early on that gender is a fundamental axis on which society is structured. It makes sense, then, that children are required to devote a great deal of time and energy to figuring out what the differences are between the gender s/he has been assigned and the 'opposite' gender. We would expect that children will attempt to draw as clear distinctions between genders as possible, as part of this process of defining themselves.

Everyday assumptions emanating from socio-biology assume that whilst children develop various behaviors through imitation and reinforcement, the basic 'blueprint' of a child's personality is already contained within the child's body and mind from birth. As an alternative to socio-biological theories, psychoanalytic theory provides one of the most enduring accounts of childhood development, arguing that early family relations structure personality. Yet both socio-biology and psychoanalytic theory focus on early differentiation between boys and girls, preferencing this differentiation as the key to understanding many later behaviors including sexual orientation, work and family relationships. These theoretical discourses are important because they provide key insights into how society accounts for gender development; that is, how much importance is attributed to biological and psychoanalytic accounts of gender development, and how this impacts on the ways in which interpersonal violence is experienced and interpreted.

Adults, rather than children, produce representations of children as innocent and gentle creatures. In this chapter I seek to critically review empirical research on childhood interpersonal violence and apply the theoretical paradigm developed in the previous chapter to map an understanding of the relationship between gender development and interpersonal violence. In order to do this, I will review research on bullying, sexual harassment in schools and sibling violence. The chapter will go on to critique research which theorizes childhood violence as the product of biology or socialization and suggest how we might employ the notions of power, investment and our knowledge of social interactions to re-interpret the dynamics of childhood interpersonal violence.

## Children's Play and Bullying

It is a commonly held view that 'play' constitutes a time in which children run around the playground, taking a break from the controlled atmosphere of the classroom. Researchers of interactions amongst children in the playground note that 'playing' actually constitutes a wide range of complex actions, in which children signal a somewhat fluid system of rules that distinguish play from non-play, often referred to as 'borderwork' (Thorne, 1993). Both in play and non-play, many children experience aggressive and violent acts directed towards them from other children within the same, or slightly older, age cohort. Indeed, most children are bullied by other children of the same age or slightly older. Younger children appear to be more at risk because of their smaller size, greater weakness and lack of experience. Bullying is a form of violence between children characterized by an imbalance of strength - either physical or psychological, between the bully and the victim; repeated negative actions against the child; and a deliberate intention to hurt the child where the violent act is largely unprovoked (Slee, 1995: 57). A number of recent studies suggest that violence in the playground and bullying make up a large percentage of child to child interpersonal violence (Olweus, 1993; Smith and Sharp, 1994). Unless the attacks lead to serious injury or are carried out by children much older than the victim, adults tend to minimize children's violent behaviors.

Dan Olweus (1984, 1985) first highlighted bullying as a serious problem for children through a massive study of 140,000 Norwegian children aged between eight and sixteen years. This study found approximately nine percent of these children were being bullied. Olweus also found that younger children were more susceptible to bullying than older children. In his study, children aged eight to twelve years reported a twelve percent rate of bullying, compared with four percent for children aged thirteen to sixteen years. In a later study, Olweus (1993) concluded that bullying was also a problem for Swedish children. In this study of 1,000 Swedish boys, four to six percent of boys aged twelve to sixteen were perceived by teachers and other children as 'extreme bullies' whilst another four to six percent of boys were 'frequent' targets of bullies.

Research elsewhere has uncovered similar findings. In England, Smith and Sharp (1994) report that twenty-three percent of the children in their study were either bullies or bullied. In a study of twenty-four schools in the Sheffield area, Ahmad, Whitney and Smith (1991) found that of the 6,758 students that took part in the study (4,135 high school and 2,623 primary/junior high), twenty-seven percent of primary school children and ten percent of high school children had been bullied more than once during the previous term. Ten percent of primary aged and four percent of the high school aged students had been bullied once or several times a week. Similarly, O'Moore and Hillery (1989) found that eight percent of the 783 Irish children studied were frequently bullied whilst thirty-four percent were occasionally bullied. Slee (1993) found that six percent of the 631 Australian primary school children studied reported being bullied an average of one to two days per week. In the United States, Perry , Kusel and Perry (1988) conducted a study of 165 school children between the ages of eight and twelve years. Perry found that ten percent of these children were classified by their classmates as extreme victims of bullying.

In all cases, the most common forms of bullying children experience are teasing, hitting and kicking. However, a wide range of bullying behaviors have been recorded including other forms of physical violence, spreading negative rumors, excluding from groups or activities, damaging belongings, having belongings stolen, being threatened and extortion.

A number of researchers recently investigated the effect bullying has on its victims. Following cases in which children have committed suicide, leaving notes or diary entries recording experiences of being bullied, it is clear that bullied children suffer emotionally from the experience. Work by Callaghan and Joseph (1995) found that children who had been bullied scored significantly higher than their non-bullied classmates on measures of depression, and lower than average with regard to self-esteem. Victims of bullying report feeling less competent in the areas of scholastic achievement, social acceptance, athletic competence, physical appearance and behavioral conduct. The effect of bullying on a child's self-esteem seems to be similar for boys and girls.[2]

One of the strongest divisions observed by children is that of gender. Children tend to play in single-gender dyads and groups and also play different games, dependent upon their gender. Observations of children on school playgrounds consistently find that boys monopolize more of the physical play space than girls (Thorne, 1993). Some researchers note that boys sometimes control as much as ten times more space than girls. Part of this finding is explained by the fact that boys' games typically take up more space than the games that girls usually play; soccer or football, for instance, require more physical space than hopscotch. Boys also invade girls' spaces more often and with less trouble. It is quite common to observe a boy running over girls' game space in order to retrieve a ball or a group of boys playing onto girls' space. However, girls are less likely than boys to complain to boys when their physical play space is invaded. The invasion of play space seems to be rather age- and gender-specific. Oswald et al. (1987) found girls and boys in the first grade of school engage in a lot of 'bothering' each other; invading physical space and teasing. By fourth grade, however, boys bother girls much more than vice versa. A significant amount of boys' 'play' involves verbal insults, physical coercion and 'play fighting' directed at girls. As they get older, girls and boys tend to avoid each other in the playground, insult one another and choose sides in games based on same-gender groups. In most research studies boys report bullying and being bullied more than girls. Boys tend to bully using physical violence whereas girls tend to use verbal violence. Girls are most often the targets of violent acts and receive more verbal insults and physical attack than do boys. Grant (1984) examined groups of first graders in an American school and found that fifty-nine percent to ninety percent of the mixed-gender aggressive instances observed involved boys aggressing against girls.

**Sexist Behavior and School Girls**

Children, from a very young age, negotiate the gender hierarchy of their society, reflected most clearly in the use of sexist behavior. In a classic study, Goodenough (1987) observed a wide range of behaviors amongst these four and five year old American children and recorded the ratio of negative to positive responses between children of same and different sexes in four kindergarten classes:

**Table 3.1        Ratios of Negative to Positive Responses for Girls and Boys in Four Kindergarten Classes**

| Group | | Boys to Boys | | Boys to Girls | | Girls to Boys | | Girls to Girls | |
|---|---|---|---|---|---|---|---|---|---|
| | | Neg. | Pos. | Neg. | Pos. | Neg. | Pos. | Neg. | Pos. |
| K1 | Resp. | 87 | 20 | 124 | 4 | 25 | 8 | 22 | 7 |
| | Ratio | 4.4 to 1 | | 31.0 to 1 | | 3.1 to 1 | | 3.1 to 1 | |
| K2 | Resp. | 80 | 32 | 32 | 51 | 17 | 46 | 19 | 44 |
| | Ratio | 2.5 to 1 | | 0.6 to 1 | | 0.37 to 1 | | 0.43 to 1 | |
| K3 | Resp. | 24 | 12 | 38 | 5 | 5 | 9 | 5 | 4 |
| | Ratio | 2.0 to 1 | | 7.6 to 1 | | 0.55 to 1 | | 1.2 to 1 | |
| K4 | Resp. | 32 | 29 | 13 | 27 | 6 | 28 | 0 | 13 |
| | Ratio | 1.1 to 1 | | 0.48 to 1 | | 0.2 to 1 | | | |
| Total | Resp. | 223 | 93 | 207 | 87 | 53 | 91 | 46 | 68 |
| | Ratio | 2.4 to 1 | | 2.4 to 1 | | 0.58 to 1 | | 0.67 to 1 | |

*Source:*      Goodenough, 1987, p.414

In the second and fourth kindergartens, the boys and girls generally got along well, and played together with low levels of aggression and put-downs. Goodenough noted these classes were made up of a core group of girls and boys who knew each other for at least one prior year. Reduced levels of cross-gender negative responses were found where both genders had been together in nursery school for a year or more. Other research concurs that familiarity with others is an important variable in children getting along with each other (Doyle, Connolly and Rivest, 1980). In the first and third kindergartens, girls did not fair so well in the company of their male classmates. Refrains of 'I hate girls' and 'girls keep out' were common. The most sexist behavior was observed in kindergarten One. The boys in this class constantly used verbal put-downs, refused to hold hands with the girls during circle games and actively resisted sitting next to girls. Boys monopolized the physical space of the classroom, broke into the play space of, and talked over, girls. As a consequence, the girls in the class seemed somewhat frightened of the boys, shadowing nearby grown-ups for protection. The girls stopped attempting to answer the teacher during question time. Goodenough reported that boys answered thirty times more questions than the girls. Some of the girls even attempted to 'buy' favor from the boys by bringing in food treats and games to give to the boys. The subsequent peace bought by these bribes lasted just until the treat was exhausted. Girls also acted in subservient ways, fetching and carrying things for the boys:

> Jill is at the sandbox with four boys. They have just taunted her and Jill chooses to ignore it. She hums a tune. Adam, coming back to the attack says, "That's a dumb song!" and Tom echoes him. Jill responds with her favorite ploy, "You're very, very smart, and you are too." Tom says with scorn, "I'm smarter than you!" Carl flies his plane close to her head, causing her to duck. Jill retaliates with, "I'm not gonna invite you to my birthday party!" Tom, complacently, "Good, you have yukky parties." Adam, "yeah!" Carl threatens again with his plane. Jill tries her mollifying tack again but can't sustain it. "Well, I am gonna invite you to my birthday party, you creeps!" Tom, in the same complacent tone, "Good!". Jill, near tears, says "Excuse me!" and leaves. Adam turns to Carl, who despite his heckling is known to like Jill and asks innocently, "Who's your best girl friend?" Carl walks into the trap, "Jill." Adam says unbelievingly, "You must be sick!" Carl quickly retreats with, "My Mom is my best friend" (Goodenough, 1987, p.421).

A number of researchers have also investigated sexual harassment of female children, particularly in the school setting (Spender, 1982). In another classic study, Herbert (1989) interviewed twelve girls in a London high school over an eight month period and found girls experienced a wide range of sexual harassment from male classmates and teachers. She also found that as the girls progressed through school their attitudes changed with regard to their academic abilities. Herbert hypothesizes that these girls learned to base their judgment of themselves according to how boys and male teachers viewed them; that their physical attributes and 'feminine' behavior counted for more than their academic achievements. Whilst lowered self-esteem is probably the result of a combination of factors, several studies of girls' adolescent development confirm that girls are reacting to a culture that perceives their ability to conform to a feminine role is essential. The fact that sexist behavior towards schoolgirls goes, for the most part, un-remarked, suggests that this behavior is most often viewed as normal, natural and undeserving of attention. Sexual harassment often goes unrecognized because a great deal of sexist and sexually harassing behavior is simply identified as 'normal'.

Sexual harassment in a school setting is difficult to recognize for two reasons. First, many behaviors that constitute sexual harassment are not defined as such by other boys and girls, teachers and school personnel. In a study conducted in London, England with fifty-one students aged twelve to sixteen years of age, the results clearly indicate that students are somewhat confused about recognizing sexual harassment (Drouet, 1993). When students were asked to identify unwanted sexual contact as 'sexual harassment', 'bullying', 'neither' or 'both', the majority (approximately ninety-seven percent of grade ten students) identified the behavior as sexual harassment compared with only a minority of grade eight students (twelve to thirteen year olds) who identified unwanted sexual touching as sexual harassment. This difference emerged again when students were asked to identify the use of verbal sexual terms. A minority of younger students identified this behavior as sexual harassment compared with a small majority of older students. Interestingly, neither the younger nor older students identified the performance of 'favors' in order to protect one's name or reputation to constitute sexual harassment. Most labeled this behavior as bullying. This is interesting given that research has found that many girls do homework, lend money, provide food or school equipment for boys in exchange for a good name or reputation (Mahoney, 1985; Drouet, 1993). Girls may also interpret sexual harassment as sanctioned in schools because they see that sexual harassment occurs with such frequency in other contexts such as public spaces (for example, the street, their mothers' work place, the bank and grocery store). Moreover, in our cultural system, girls and boys are taught that girls should be flattered by male attention. We teach girls that male comments about their bodies demonstrate that boys and male teachers 'asppreciate' girls' appearance.

**Sibling Violence**

Since violence between siblings (usually) involves biologically related individuals, this form of interpersonal violence is strictly beyond the theme of this book, which focuses on non-biologically related individuals. It is mentioned here for two reasons. First, it makes up a significant proportion of the violence in childhood. Second, it is mainly considered 'normal' in Western society and has consequently received little attention. We tend to think that conflict between brothers and sisters is both commonplace and a 'normal' part of growing up. Indeed, many parents think that fighting with siblings teaches children how to 'stand up for themselves'. However, there is more to sibling violence than simply learning the lessons of life through innocent 'tiffs' with sisters and brothers.

Although under-researched, it appears that sibling violence constitutes one of the major forms of 'family violence'. In a pioneering study on the subject Steinmetz (1977b) found that sibling violence was more common than wife assault or child abuse. The results of this study indicated that sibling violence ranges in form from verbal attacks to extreme violence.

Steinmetz found that eighty-two percent of the fifty-seven families interviewed reported at least one violent incident in the past year. Fifty-three percent of these families reported serious physical violence such as kicking, biting, punching, hitting with an object and beating. It does appear that as children age, they become less violent towards their siblings. Boys seem to be slightly more violent than their sisters. In fact, having a sister in the family helps to reduce the amount of sibling violence; and families with only sons reported more sibling violence. Interestingly, the amount and severity of sibling violence does not seem to depend on the number of children in the family. However, much of the detail of this form of interpersonal violence requires research.

**Theorizing Childhood Interpersonal Violence: Biology versus Social Construction**

Beyond prevalence and incidence estimations, most research on childhood violence tends to focus on the supposed difference that gender makes in determining levels of violence. That is, research tends to focus on violence committed by male children and explains this violence as either innate or developed through a simple process of imitation and positive reinforcement. In the continuing tension between biological and sociological theories, the presence of violence during childhood takes on particular salience. Consistent evidence that boys are more aggressive from infancy would lend support a biological basis of violence. Indeed, whilst we might be willing to conclude that adult males are more violent than females because of a complex interaction of investment in particular practices of masculinity, this argument is less persuasive when applied to a six month old boy.

Most research concerned with a biological etiology of childhood violence focus primarily on hormone and chromosome differences between boys and girls, as well as observation of children's displays of aggression.[3] But in a comprehensive review of the few studies actually correlating hormone levels with aggression, Fausto-Sterling (1992) sheds light on the theory that aggression is biologically determined. Most studies in this area measure differences in testosterone levels between violent and non-violent men.[4] These studies are limited by their failure to sample females as well as males, but more importantly, none of the studies suggest a causal relationship between testosterone level and aggression. At least three studies repeating these experiments concluded no correlation between testosterone and aggression.[5]

Similarly, studies investigating aberrations in sex chromosome assignment, such as boys who are born with an extra Y chromosome (XYY) have found no consistent link between chromosomes and levels of aggression (Jacobs et al., 1965; Witkin et al., 1983). Other studies have examined cases in which human fetuses were exposed to hormones (Money and Ehrhardt, 1972). In some cases, drugs were administered to pregnant women, exposing their babies to abnormally high levels of hormones. In these studies, mothers reported their androgenized female children displayed higher levels of 'tomboy' behavior. This behavior included more 'rough' play, a preference for toy cars and guns to dolls and a greater focus on career than marriage. Although this and similar studies suffer from a number of limitations, the most relevant point to make here is that parents and researchers alike determined *a priori* certain behaviors as feminine and other behaviors as masculine, and then determined the gender 'appropriateness' of the children from this determination. This point will be returned to later in this section.

Socialization theory, by contrast, rejects arguments that violence is innate and argues instead that differences in the ways in which girls and boys are raised effect levels of violence (Miedzian, 1991). From birth, girls and boys are treated differently. Boys are picked up more often, talked to more and encouraged to physically move more often. Boys receive more physical punishment than do girls. Female infants are kept closer to their caregivers, not encouraged to move as freely and talked to more (Lorber, 1994). At the public level, the forms of masculinity and femininity advocated for boys and girls are openly displayed. For instance, store signs delineating girls' and boys' toys are unnecessary and few toys are intentionally unisex. Girls' toys have pink and powder blue boxes. Blonde, white girls play happily with super-model Barbie dolls, tea sets and little ponies. Girls can feed, change diapers, walk, dress and bathe dolls of various sizes. They can pretend to cook in make-believe ovens, learn to braid hair and nurse pretend people back to health. Girls' toys remain fastened to the notion of females as caregivers and the toys designated for girls prepare them for careers in the 'caring professions' such as nurses and mothers. Boys' aisles, in contrast, are filled with enough pretend arsenal to rival the best Swiss Army mountain base. There are guns of every description with which boys are encouraged to practice aggressive behavior.

Socialization theory provides a strong case concerning the structural context within which individuals negotiate their experiences of gender performance. Clearly, parents, siblings, peers and schools and other institutions all present powerful examples of 'appropriate' gender performance, and those behaviors which society will sanction. On the other hand, socialization theory does not lend itself very readily to theorizing the individual agency required to negotiate social relations. Simply playing with certain toys does not 'produce' violent children. Nor is it true that children raised in gender stereotyped ways necessarily grow up to display traditionally 'feminine' or 'masculine' characteristics. Most of us can readily bring to mind examples of people we know who were raised in particular ways and yet grew up to behave quite differently. Quite commonly we hear mothers and fathers say that although they, for the most part, raised their sons and daughters in the same way, it is their sons who prefer to play 'cops and robbers' and their daughters who prefer to play co-operative, home-oriented games such as 'dress-up'.

It may be suggested that children interpret a very complex combination of explicit, subtle and often conflicting messages about what appears to constitute 'appropriate' gendered behavior. Each child negotiates these messages, and children's behavior represents the process and outcome of this negotiation. The genders which children perform are thus highly context-dependent. It may be argued that those boys and girls who act violently do not do so because they have a preference (innate or socialized) to play with 'violent' toys which in turn socialize them to further violence. Boys and girls who act violently do so as the result of a process of individual negotiation. These boys and girls observe violence, practice violence and learn to use violence. If this is so, it remains to extrapolate what this 'practice' constitutes for children and how children practice gender and the system on which gender practice is based.

Psychoanalytic theories provide the most detailed arguments concerning early child development, and each is predicated on the invocation of a binary to define gender. Sigmund Freud developed a systematic theory of human development through observation (primarily in the form of case studies) and interpretation. Hitherto, little attention had been paid to gender, or gender difference, and certainly not its construction within a social milieu. Fore fronting the association between gender, sexuality and identity, Freud (1901) maintained that humans are born 'polymorphously perverse', a radical departure from the innate and self-evident sexuality of previous theoretical conceptions. Freud is most popularly known for his development of the 'Oedipus Complex', borrowed from the Greek tragedy. Freud theorized that the infant boy craves the satisfaction of an undeveloped yet powerful inherent sexual drive. A crucial phase in the development of masculinity occurs when young boys direct this sexual desire towards their mothers. The presence of the father prevents the satisfaction of the boy's desires and, moreover, invokes a threat of castration as punishment for the boy's desire. The development of 'normal' masculinity is predicated on the boy's successful association with the father, rejection of his mother (and femininity) and eventual satisfaction of sexual desires through heterosexuality. Though caricatured beyond sensibility in its popular interpretation, Freud's theory of male development needs to be credited with a number of innovations. Firstly, Freud introduces the very notion of gender development: individuals are not born with an innately pre-formed gender or sexuality. Secondly, the environment, or more centrally culture, profoundly shapes the forms of gender identity. In this important sense, gender identity is not static; rather, it exists as a multi-layered lived experience, with possibilities for growth and transformation.

In its various evolutions, psychoanalytic theory has tended to focus more on the supposed necessary transitions to 'normal' heterosexual development, reflecting the general political and social orthodoxy of the times. A great deal of this work was concerned with the dyfunctionalizing of homosexuality, marking heterosexuality as the 'normal' and preferred path of male development. Freud's (1901) theory of child development has undergone a myriad of transformations, particularly in the works of Lacan's (1977) symbolic order, Erikson's (1951) ego-identity development, Jung's (1953) archetypes and deBeauvoir's (1972) adaptation of Sartre's (1965) existentialism to the development of the self in social relation.

One particularly compelling twist to psychoanalytic theories of gender development is presented in the work of Nancy Chodorow (1978, 1989) who found male, as opposed to female, development to be problematic. Whilst traditional psychoanalytic theory considers the reconciliation of female's sexual desire as problematic because of the 'lack' of phallus, Chodorow argues that most children are raised with a female (most often the mother) as the central object of relation. Thus it is not girls who must engage in the task of separation from this primary relationship, since girls reproduce the 'institution' of motherhood. Rather it is boys who face the daunting task of learning their gender through differentiation from the maternal figure. The supposed difficulty that males have for developing and maintaining intimacy is traced to the necessary emplacement by the boy of boundaries between himself and his mother.[6]

One of the most developed analyses to emanate from Freudian psychoanalytic theory is the work of Jacques Lacan (1977). Lacan postulated that each society regulates itself through a 'Symbolic Order' which designates the totality of signs, roles, norms and rituals of that society. Children only learn how to live in the world both through their acquisition and internalization of this Symbolic Order. Whatever constancy is maintained in society is achieved through each individual's unconscious internalization of the language of society, a language that regulates individuals.[7] The language of the Symbolic Order includes specific gender 'signs'. That is, boys and girls experience the Symbolic Order differently. The father represents the powerful, phallic, Symbolic Order: the word. The mother, through the process of self-identification, has emerged as the Other. For boys, their identification with their fathers means a complete internalization of the Symbolic Order. Girls, on the other hand, do not identify with their fathers and never fully internalize the Symbolic Order: indeed, girls are *excluded* from the Symbolic Order, relegated to the margins.[8]

Lacan's theory of the Symbolic Order has been criticized for it's over emphasis on the spoken word and its phallocentrism.[9] What is important to this analysis, however, is that Lacan, Freud and other central psychoanalytic theorists invoke a language of binaries to explain child development. It is within poststructualism and postmodernism, in the works of Jacques Derrida (1978) for instance, that this insistence on binaries is deconstructed. According to Derrida, language does not actually constitute meaning: language can only partially *create* and *represent* the meaning of anything. Derrida referred to the gap between the reality of the object and our perception of that object as 'difference'. Gender is given meaning through difference.

In attempting to learn and negotiate their own subjectivities, children are keen identifiers of the mechanisms through which gender difference is articulated. These mechanisms include such things as how to walk and talk, how to dress, what to say, when to listen, how to play and what to play. Because gender is such an obvious marker in society, I argue that children use gender as a major guide for interpreting how they can and are expected to negotiate their social relations and environments. Children and their caregivers are engaged in a continuous process of active negotiation in which caregivers and children respond to each other as gendered individuals.[10] This is unsurprising given that our society almost exclusively focuses on sustaining differences *between* genders (Miedzian, 1991; Lorber, 1994).

As Chapter Two argued, the hegemonic, heterosexual masculine ideal is configured in such as way as to be necessarily positioned above all other masculinities, as well as all femininities. In order to maintain this positioning, heterosexual masculinity must constantly maintain distance (difference) from femininity. A number of theorists argue this is the case because heterosexual masculinity is more valued than femininity.[11] This means that particular importance will be placed on the learning of heterosexual masculinity. There is some evidence to suggest that while girls are afforded some leeway in their behaviors, boys' behaviors are more closely monitored (Maccoby and Jacklin, 1974). Caregivers are vigilantly watching for signs that their son displays appropriate 'masculine' behaviors. Girls may get away with being 'tomboys' for a few early years, but few boys are encouraged to behave as 'sissies'. The primary means by which boys learn heterosexual masculinity is through practice. As heterosexual masculinity is predicated on superiority over women, boys practice behaviors which treat girls as inferior.

An essential component of heterosexual masculinity is the ability to demonstrate a preference for aggressive and emotionally distant games (Lorber, 1994). Much cross-gender aggressive play emphasizes the two genders as different and in opposition. When caregivers dismiss boys' violence with 'boys will be boys' and 'he pulls girls' hair because he likes girls' they are practicing the dominant heterosexual masculinity. Indeed, when boys engage in this type of behavior many caregivers are reassured that their sons are 'normal' and not too 'feminine'.

Some studies suggest an association between parental attitudes towards sons and their sons later involvement with violence. In their classic study, Bandura and Walters (1959) examined the families of boys who displayed neither aggression nor passivity and those boys who were repeatedly antisocially aggressive. They found, not surprisingly, that parents of non-aggressive boys reinforced non-aggressive methods of problem resolution and depended, themselves, on reasoning to resolve their own problems. Parents of aggressive boys, on the other hand, consistently taught their sons to use physically aggressive strategies. Violence against their parents was not allowed, but teachers, peers and other adults were permissible targets for their sons' aggression. These parents reported concern that their sons do not become 'feminized'. In a society dependent upon a binary conception of gender and committed to heterosexuality as the preferable subjectivity, the boy who displays 'feminine' behavior will be positioned below boys who display 'masculine' behaviors. In an effort to ensure that their sons are not subjected to the consequences of not displaying 'appropriate' heterosexual masculinity, many parents encourage aggressive behavior as a readily identified behavior associated with masculinity.

Girls and boys are concerned about aggressive boys, but boys are also concerned about 'feminized' boys. In a provocative study of child attitudes, Boulton and Underwood (1992) asked children why bullies pick on other children. Not surprisingly, the largest percentage of victims reported that they had been bullied because they were smaller or weaker than the bully. Most victims and bullies reported that bullies felt happy, clever, strong and tough after bullying another child. It appears that male bullies receive some respect from peers for their behavior. Children interpret bullying as an active means of obtaining some desired object as well as evidence, and a consequence, of greater strength. But boys also report that male bullies are fulfilling a valued masculine role. That is, boys who use violence are demonstrating that they are able to perform the hegemonic heterosexual masculinity: these boys are 'real' men. Indeed, most children report that they understand why bullies act the way they do.

It is important to understand these findings, not in terms of gender differences grounded in biology, but as children's attempts to understand and negotiate their environments, and particularly their social relations with others. One of the most keenly observed markers in our highly complex societies is gender and it is not surprising that children fix on this marker early in order to facilitate their learning. Bauman (1997) applies his insights into the ways in which social boundaries are created and maintained to ethnic and racial relations. However, it is clear that this analysis may be brought to bear on the making of gender as well. Using the insights of the phenomenologist Alfred Shutz, Bauman observes:

> If we humans may "find our bearings within our natural and socio-cultural environment and to come to terms with it", it is thanks to the fact that this environment has been "preselected and preinterpreted...by a series of common-sense constructs of the reality of daily life". Without such knowledge, living in the world would be inconceivable. None of us is able to build the world of significations and meanings from scratch; each of us enters a "prefabricated" world (1997, p.8).

As poststructuralists have observed, our very language is structured through binaries, and sexual difference provides one of the key binaries used to differentiate 'like' from 'unlike'. Children are required to learn how they are expected to behave in an increasing number of contexts: first in the family, then at school and with other children and adults. Children thus actively respond to their own need to order their complex environments, and the signals provided by those around them to differentiate on the basis of gender. The research reviewed earlier strongly suggests that children's interactions in the playground are highly structured by gender, with children largely interacting with members of their own gender. The repeated observation that boys claim more space than girls, invade girls' space more frequently, interrupt girls' play, and bully girls more often is less the product of biology and more the case of boys *acting* their gender.

Boys who bully girls and other boys, and are sexist towards girls, are attempting to perform a particularly valued masculinity. Bullying and sexist behavior is a means by which boys attempt to establish their superiority over girls, which in our society means to *be* masculine. It also marks the beginnings of boys' fumblings towards heterosexuality, which offers a highly structured relation between women and men.

## Notes

1     Childhood may be defined as the period from birth to adolescence, roughly from zero to thirteen years.

2     Many schools in several countries are actively tackling the problem of bullying. In the United Kingdom, as a result of the Elton Report (H.M.S.O., 1989) *Discipline in Schools* in which bullying was acknowledged to have a considerable 'damaging effect' on children, a number of schools have launched anti-bullying programs. Parents have formed action groups such as the Anti-Bullying Campaign. School strategies include developing policies that explicitly outlaw bullying, teaching about bulling in the curriculum, involving students through such alternatives as 'buddy systems' in which older children pair up with younger children. Older children can provide their younger 'buddies' with strategies to deal with bullies and to protect themselves by reporting bullying to teachers and parents. Older children have also directly intervened in some cases where their younger 'buddy' was being bullied. As a result of Olweus's study, the Norwegian government began a national campaign in 1983 to end bullying in primary and junior high schools. Guidance booklets, videos, story books and teaching packs are all methods of addressing the problem of bullying.

3     Much has been written about dominance hierarchies in animal species. Many studies conclude that these hierarchies are context-dependent. That is, when monkeys and other vertebrates are held in captivity, they tend to establish hierarchies which do not exist in the wild (Rowell, 1972, 1974; Fedigan, 1982). And the hierarchies that do exist do not appear to be consistent. For instance, Ardrey (1967) found that while monkeys may dominate with regard to sexual behavior those same monkeys are submissive with regard to aggression displays. One popularly assumed 'fact' with regard to animal hierarchies is that dominant males (that is males of higher rank) have first choice of mating with ovulating females. But amongst scientists, it is known that the evidence is, in fact, mixed. Some studies have found that females exert much more control in choosing their mating partners (see for example, Kolata, 1976). Studies using biochemical tests to determine the paternity of offspring have found that low ranking males were as likely, or more likely, to father offspring as their high ranking 'competitors'. No direct correlation between male dominance ranking and paternity has been established. More general evidence concerning dominance of males over females in primate populations has also proved ambiguous (Rowell, 1974). In some animals, such as forest-dwelling baboons, it is females who form the core, stable group and determine group movements throughout the forest. Strong male baboons are the first to climb trees for safety when the group is startled. Females are left to fend for themselves encumbered with their children. Many zoological and biological studies of animals have been criticized on methodological grounds. Some have suggested that these studies are biased in that the researchers assume that

aggressiveness is a male quality. This assumption might lead researchers to look for instances of male aggression more often, record these instances more frequently and label more male behaviors as aggressive.

4     Fausto-Sterling (1992) contends that there may not be more than six actual studies of this kind.

5     Stress has been found to lower testosterone levels. The armies of the past, (whose men actually faced each other on the battlefield) would have shown lower than normal levels of testosterone, as with animals. Most studies of male primates have demonstrated no correlation between testosterone levels and placement in a dominance hierarchy. One study (Rose, Gordon, and Bernstein, 1972) actually found that the most dominant male in the group has the lowest testosterone level. These studies now suggest that the direction of the relationship between hormones and dominance might be incorrect. That is, we have usually assumed that testosterone levels determine dominance. But perhaps it is the other way around. Some researchers have found that social context determines testosterone level. When faced with a receptive female, male testosterone levels increase. Faced, on the other hand, with a group of attackers, male testosterone levels decrease (Rose, Gordon and Bernstein, 1972).

6     This analysis has more recently been taken up by a number of psychoanalytic feminists including Hollway (1995).

7     Lacan goes on to outline a modified version of Freud's developmental stages. In the first pre-Oedipal phase, the 'Imaginary Phase', the child has no understanding (or inkling) of the Symbolic Order. Male and female children have no ego boundaries, being completely unaware of where their body ends and their mother's body begins. Until the child is born, s/he is not physically separate from the mother, made by her body and joined by the umbilical cord. In the second part of the Imaginary Phase the child learns to recognize her/himself as a self, distinct from her/his mother. This phase is crucial to our concept of self. Imagine an infant being held up to a mirror by her/his mother. At first the child does not recognize the image in the mirror, but gradually learns to distinguish between her/himself and the mirror image. In other words, the self only understands itself *by the reflection* of the Other. In the final 'Oedipal' phase, the child recognizes that s/he is completely separate from the mother: indeed, she has become Other.

8     The creation of woman as Other and its consequences for the oppression of women is the main subject of Simone deBeauvoir's *The Second Sex* (1953).

9     Irigaray (1985a, 1985b) provides one of the most sustained critiques of the phallocentrism in psychoanalysis.

10    It is useful here to remember that parents, siblings, extended family, teachers, friends and children themselves are not practicing *a* particular masculinity or femininity but are negotiating between a number of available subject positions. Different masculinities and femininities will be preferred over others, depending on the unique configuration of the family and their social environment.

11    Weeks (1986) furthers this argument by suggesting that 'compulsory heterosexuality' sustains the family as the fundamental unit on which our socio-economic system relies by hierarchically positioning heterosexuality (and heterosexuals) over all other forms of sexuality.

# Chapter 4

# Heteronormativity and Sexual Coercion: Adolescents Practicing Gender

The discussion of childhood interpersonal violence in the previous chapter suggests that children are involved in a complex process of learning how to practice gender. Children are exposed to discourses that manufacture a set of oppositional relations between masculinity and femininity (Kelly, 1984; Richardson, 1996). These discourses define heterosexual masculinity as active, fearless, rational and autonomous; and femininity as passive, irrational, emotional and dependent.

Adolescence is a particularly important period of physical development and sexual exploration, a time when concern with intimacy and sexual relations is often brought to the fore. Young women and men are under pressure to negotiate a set of normative conceptions and expectations concerning sexuality. These conceptions involve particular understandings of masculinity and femininity, sexual reputations and desire. Although individual adolescents provide varying accounts of this negotiation, I will argue in this chapter that the normative structure of heterosexuality can be traced such that gender identity forefronts this process. That is, to become sexually active, adolescents necessarily encounter gendered power relations. 'Normal' heterosexuality is predicated on a conceptualisation of masculinity as active, persistent and powerful, and femininity as passive, receptive and responsive to male sexuality.

Further, heteronormativity critically informs conceptions of male sexuality. These include the belief that men's heterosexuality is biologically derived, that men persistently desire sex, that the desire to engage in sexual activity is always towards an 'end goal' of coitus and ejaculation, and that this inherent need to engage in sexual intercourse prompts males to always initiate sexual activity with women. This biologically driven discourse of male sexuality contemporaneously operates beside a discourse of compulsory heterosexuality (Hollway, 1989). Kimmel (1997) and Connell (1995) argue that heterosexual sex is a primary means of establishing masculinity. Female sexuality, on the other hand, is particularly configured in terms of absence. When women's sexuality is considered at all, it is as though it is complex and vague: women do not initiate sexual activity and require sustained sexual stimulation to become aroused; but once aroused, women's desire become insatiable (Burt and Albin, 1981; Tiefer, 1987).

The importance of first heterosexual experience as a product of the normative construction of heterosexuality is illustrated in Holland et al.'s (1996) study of young men and women's descriptions of their first experience of sexual intercourse. Holland et al. contend that 'first sex' is the most significant marker through which young men become men.[1] This study shows the importance of male peer groups which mutually reinforce sexual intercourse with women as signifier of both heterosexuality and masculinity. First intercourse was defined as a wholly male concern; women's 'power' was significantly defined in terms of her possible refusal of his advances. Indeed, we would argue that this possibility of refusal forms a central concern for women within a heteronormative system, as the non-desiring (read 'good') woman is always responsible for saying 'no'.

Female adolescents' 'first sex' often takes place within the context of 'first love' relationships. Accordingly adolescents draw on the intertwining discourses of romance and sexuality available to them in the wider culture. I will argue that romantic discourse affirms a traditionally feminine identity, exemplified in passivity, emotionality and dependency. Placing romantic discourse within the hegemonic structure of Western society helps to explain why romantic, traditionally feminine constructions of self prevail over alternatives (Connell, 1995).

A growing body of theoretical and empirical research has illuminated the link between normative conceptions and expectations concerning female and male sexuality, and sexual coercion. By interrogating beliefs about 'normal' male and female sexuality, the ways in which sexual coercion is configured as a normal part of heterosexual relationships can be traced. Sexual stereotyping by contemporary heterosexual ideology arguably sustains antagonistic relations between women and men. Women's sexuality is considered complex compared with the simplicity of men's constant desire for coitus. This means that men will always initiate sexual activity, to which women will only reluctantly respond positively. Hence the common belief that men should make sexual advances persistently whilst women should always only react to male volition. So when women say 'no', they really mean 'yes'.

**Adolescent Dating Violence**

Because most individuals perceive interpersonal violence as an 'adult' problem, violence in adolescent relationships is not easily identified; and, indeed, violence in adolescent relationships has only recently begun to be studied. Mainly emanating from North America,[2] research suggests that aggression in late adolescence is at least as prevalent as wife assault (see for example Mercer, 1986; Muehlenhard and Linton, 1987; Stets and Pirog-Good, 1987; DeKeseredy, 1988; Follingstad et al. 1991 and; Lloyd, 1991). The FBI estimates that twenty percent of female homicide victims are between the ages of fifteen and twenty-four (Spaid, 1993). We have seen that most women are killed by their (ex)partners. An early study of American university students found that one in five heterosexual dating relationships featured physical aggression (Makepeace, 1981). Similar studies found between a third (Stets and Henderson, 1991) to one half of adolescent girls had experienced dating aggression (Barnes et al., 1991).

Two separate studies conducted in the United States (Henton et al., 1983; Kutner, 1991) observed that fifty percent of all young girlfriends remained with their young boyfriends after they had been abused. It was also found that these adolescents' parents were rarely aware of the violence taking place (Kutner, 1991). Similarly, a study of secondary students reported that sixty-six percent of the young women would tell friends about the abuse, twenty percent would tell no one, but only eight percent would tell their parents, eight percent would tell a sibling, six percent would tell a teacher or counselor and a mere two percent would inform the police (Burcky, Reuterman and Kopsky, 1988).

*Psychological Violence*

Continuing the elaboration of the ways in which gender informs our understandings and practices of interpersonal violence, this chapter focuses on adolescent dating violence. The narratives on which this analysis is based were drawn from a study I conducted of adolescent heterosexual dating violence in the United Kingdom (see Hird, 1995b, 2000a; Hird and Jackson, 2001). The study took place within the context of growing awareness of the high rates of interpersonal violence in adolescent heterosexual dating relationships.[3] I will particularly focus on those narratives that considered sexuality and sexual practices within the context of 'normal' heterosexual sexuality experienced as coercive by female adolescents. This chapter extends the aim of this book which is to argue that particular discourses on gender polarize masculinity and femininity and that this polarization conditions heterosexual interpersonal violence.

Psychological violence refers to intimidating, terrorizing, humiliating, insulting, isolating the person from family and/or friends, yelling and/or screaming at the person in order to induce fear, destroying the person's property or controlling the person's movements (Jukes, 1993). The most frequent form of psychological violence found in this study was name-calling. The most frequently used words were 'slag', 'tart' and 'bit' which referred to a girl's sexual behavior; either sexual promiscuity or frigidity:

| | |
|---|---|
| Myra | Do you call guys names? |
| Elicia | Bastards. That's about it. There isn't a male version of slag. I mean you just say whatever describes him. |
| Myra | Why is that? |
| Elicia | It is easier for blokes to put girls... |
| Emma | Into boxes. |
| Myra | Why? |
| Elicia | Because of the stereotypes there are? If she's clever then she's "square" and if she's friendly she's a "flirt" and she's a "slag". |

Reference to boys' sexuality in negative terms occurred when boys were referred to as homosexuals with such terms as 'fag' and 'poof'. As Kimmel (1996) and Connell (1995) have argued, hegemonic masculinity is premised on the denial of femininity,which is conflated with homosexuality. Sexual relationships provide an important proving ground for boys to dispel any association with femininity or homosexuality. In this study heterosexual sex was seen by the young men as a means of disproving homosexuality (and subsequently all that might be considered feminine). Male peers served as a form of sexual police, cajoling, teasing and tirelessly asking about one another's sexual 'scores'.

Other forms of psychological violence reportedly used by both boys and girls were verbal put-down other than name-calling and controlling behavior. For instance, these two young men described their girlfriends' use of psychologically controlling behavior:

But if I do mention a girl's name, she'll hate them. She scribbled her name and number out of my address book. And that kind of thing annoyed me but she's allowed to be immature and she said oh I'm only joking but now she's got rid of the number and I can't (call the girl) so she may have been joking but she got rid of it which is what she was intending.

You know I mentioned I went on holiday with another girl? Well I have this picture of us and Kathy didn't like that and she just ripped it up and ripped my little head out of it and threw it on the floor with my head missing and I said "what are you doing" and she said "you don't want it there anymore, why do you want it there?". And I said "I've got pictures of football players up there as well" and she said "that's different".

Thus the most frequently cited form of psychological violence in my study seemed to occur with about equal frequency for young men and women. That is, it appears that levels of psychological violence committed by males and females is more equal than physical and sexual forms of interpersonal violence.

*Physical Violence*

Physical acts such as slapping, hitting and punching were described as a 'normal' and familiar part of adolescent relationships. Most girls reported being hit, held down, slapped, kicked or punched by their boyfriends. Boys also talked about girls who were physically violent towards them. Sarah described a typical experience of physical violence. During a 'play-fight', her boyfriend sat on top of Sarah on the bed. He held both of her arms above her head. When she realized that she could not move him off her, she told him to let her go. But he continued to hold her until she showed that she was upset and yelled at him to get off her. This small incident resulted in bruises on Sarah's wrists and a pulled muscle in her shoulder from her efforts to be released. Sarah said that she was quite disturbed by the incident. Until that time, she had not considered that her boyfriend could ever harm her:

I just couldn't understand how he could do that. I trusted him so much. I trusted him completely. I trusted him more in a relationship than I had trusted anyone before.

There were also a number of discussions of female violence. However, most of girls' reported physical violence was actually self-defence against their boyfriends' use of physical and/or sexual violence. Gillian explained:

someone I know got pushed against this wall by this bloke at a party and he was like pushing himself against her kind of thing and she hit him and I think that's exactly what she should have done...even if he hadn't gone any further he was still doing something that she didn't want and she made it clear that she didn't want it. And he didn't take any notice so she hit him. And I think that's what I would have done really. I hope I would have done that.

The importance of recognising the meaning of aggressive acts was further provided in accounts of the physical consequences of aggressive actions. Girls and boys agreed that a boy *hitting* a girl was 'worse' than a girl *punching* a boy because the boy's greater strength would do greater harm.

However, some of the violence described was neither defensive nor retaliatory. For instance, Kate described feelings of intense anger when her boyfriend would not do what she wanted. On several occasions she reported having hit him on the face and head. She had also kicked and punched him:

> It wasn't good and he was really pissing me off and I couldn't find a way to react and he was upsetting me and he didn't realize how much he was upsetting me and I slapped him in the face. And I hit him as hard as I could...men have violent feelings but so do women. There are some times when I just really, really want to hit people. Sometimes I just get really angry and aggressive and I see Mark and I just find an excuse to argue and hit him.

## Sexual Violence

Almost all girls in the study reported being either pressured, coerced or actually forced to have sexual intercourse with a male adolescent or adult. The most commonly experienced form of sexual violence was unwanted sexual touching. Sexual violence was almost exclusively perpetrated by young men known to the girls as acquaintances, friends or boyfriends. Instances of sexual violence most often took place on dates, at social events such as parties or in the homes of either boy or girl. Krista's account suggests how some sexual violence often occurs in adolescent dating relationships. Krista was fifteen and had been dating her first boyfriend, Ned, for several months. For some time he had been pressuring her to have sex. One night Krista and Ned were walking in a badly lit, deserted park. Ned attempted to have sex with Krista, who refused:

> Krista    It was really, really dark and he took my top off and he said that if I didn't have sex with him he would finish with me. And I thought "what do I do, what do I do? I don't want to finish with him but I really, really don't want to have sex". And he started having sex with me and I started feeling sick and scared. And there had been loads of times when we had just spent the whole night getting off and kissing and he had always stopped and said "I had better go because you are really turning me on and I know you don't want to".

| Myra | Why did you feel scared? |
| Krista | Just because that was the one thing that I really did not want to do. I was totally out of control. And he started shouting at me and he was angry it was like he had flipped and I knew he was very emotionally mixed up and I knew that he would never be able to love just because of how he had been raised and brought up and passed around by so many people. |
| Myra | So what happened? |
| Krista | He walked off but he came back. I think he knew he would have to stop me being upset so that I didn't go back to everyone and say what a bastard he was which is what I would have done and he knew this and so he started telling me that there was this girl after him and she was blonde and was perfect. I think he just really wanted to hurt me. And he just sort of got on top of me and it was over before I knew it. I was so scared. |

This incident of sexual violence resulted in Krista's pregnancy. Through Ned's boasting, many of the students in the school found out that Krista was pregnant. In her distress, Krista failed her final exams. Krista later found out that Ned raped his next girlfriend.

Rose was raped repeatedly during her relationship with David. She described the context:

| Rose | If I just went to him just for a cuddle it would always turn into sex. And I would sort of like say "no, no I don't want to" and he'd force me and I'd cry and say "I just wanted a cuddle, I didn't want sex". |
| Myra | How do you mean he'd force you? |
| Rose | He would sometimes pressure me into sex because...he wanted to basically, so...he was stronger than me and... |
| Myra | He actually physically forced you? |
| Rose | Yeah, and there were quite a few times that he forced me. All of a sudden he was sort of...it's like he went into, like he blacked out or something, he would become very aggressive. Cause I'd be crying and saying "I don't wanna. Get off" and so if you think it is rape, really, if I say no. And he would sort of think "shit, what have I done". I think in a way he mistook my actions, like I'd go to him for a cuddle, and that's all I wanted, but he got the wrong impression. And at the end of the day it's wrong for him to do that and I know it's wrong and still don't forgive him for that. |

## Interpreting Adolescent Interpersonal Violence

This data concurs with a growing number of studies that suggest dating violence is a prevalent and serious problem for adolescents. I now turn to an analysis of the narratives concerned with stranger sexual violence and the context and meaning of dating violence to argue that adolescents primarily use a discourse of biological essentialism to explain their experiences of interpersonal violence.

### *Acquaintance versus Stranger Sexual Violence*

As the first chapter argued, women are much more likely to be victims of interpersonal violence than violence committed by strangers. This means that women are most likely to personally know their assailants. An excellent example of the ways in which women experience interpersonal violence and yet focus on stranger violence was provided in the discussions by young women. Most young women related narratives of sexual violence committed by strangers. A man walked by one woman, grabbing her and kissing her. Two young women were followed home and the man stood outside the house for approximately half an hour after they had run inside the house. Another young woman had an older man stop her and ask the time. He followed her down the street, ran up behind her, grabbed her and put his hand on her breast. Most young women talked about being whistled at and commented on by various male strangers.

However, these young women actually experienced most sexual violence from the young men they knew. The types and severity of violence varied significantly as the following excerpts suggest. For instance, Sandra described an incident in which she had male and female friends sleeping overnight in her room. She woke up in the night to find her male friend touching her breasts with his hands. She described her reaction:

I was just so embarrassed by the whole situation I just lay there and didn't say anything. And now I just feel so pathetic for not doing anything. I told my friend Debbie about it and she said "well, why in the hell didn't you stop him?" But the fact that I liked him so much and it really upset me. First of all I couldn't figure out what was going on cause I didn't know why I had woken up and then it had been a while and he had put his hand back again. And I tried, I literally opened my mouth to say something and no words came out. So it would look like I had let him for a bit and then stopped him. And then a few days later he was talking to Debbie about how he was really into getting off with young women with big tits and stuff...I just felt sick.

These young women did not immediately relate these experiences to discussions of personal safety. Indeed, these women were very comfortable in talking about the danger imposed by strangers but quite uncomfortable when the discussion turned to young men that they knew. The young women did not link interpersonal violence with protecting themselves from their male friends and boyfriends. Indeed, when I queried this lack of connection, several of the young women became upset:

> Linda    It happened a year ago [referring to a male friend who attempted to rape her] and it's like I've blocked it out. I don't want to think about it. Not all young men are like that I think.
>
> Harriet   But the interesting thing is that even if he isn't the type and he wouldn't do that, he could. Since it happened to me I haven't actually thought about it until now when you have sort of got me to think about it again.
>
> Elicia    I think we do that in a way because it's less frightening. I can cope with the fear of being attacked by a stranger in a way it's something you can believe. You understand that an insane stranger would want to attack you. But you cannot understand how your boyfriend who is supposed to love you, protect you and like you could do that to you. That's terrifying. And I also think "well, what can I do about it? Can I actually do anything in a relationship?" You can be in a relationship and always surround yourself with people but that wouldn't be a relationship. You can think of things like take a taxi and stuff but it won't protect you from your boyfriend.

Young women reported that they could not control stranger rape and were therefore not responsible for this form of violence (or would not be blamed). Date rape was associated with a strong degree of responsibility in preventing the young man's action:

> We're more frightened of being raped on the street because they [females] know they have no control over it. It's because they are a woman on the street [that] they are raped. It's not because they are out with this man or they know this man. Whereas if they are with this man at least they should try to control the situation and communicate with this man. And they know their relationship...Whereas on the street they are just another woman and that's why they are victims and they have so little control over that. There is nothing they can do about it.

Talk about measures taken to protect themselves from stranger rape suggests, paradoxically, that young women do attempt to exert some kind of control over stranger rape. This is interesting given that these young women talked about stranger rape as 'uncontrollable' and date rape as 'controllable' (that is, preventable through their own actions). Further analysis suggests that what these young women are actually talking about is the likelihood of being blamed for rape. If a woman takes 'reasonable' precautions against stranger rape (such as not walking down ill-lit paths at night), then she can say that she was not responsible for the rape. Moreover, because her rapist is a stranger, she feels people are less likely to believe that she wanted to engage in sexual intercourse with a stranger. The assessment that a woman did not consent to sexual intercourse is less likely when she knows her rapist, is at his apartment and agreed earlier to go out on a date with him. When the young women in this study talked about responsibility, therefore, they were really talking about how people would apportion blame. Young women adamantly resisted talking about the potential threat posed by male friends. Because these friendships were wholly dependent on the assumption that these young men would not abuse their female friends' trust.

I detail at some length these young women's discussions of stranger and known interpersonal sexual violence because they highlight some of the most common assumptions held concerning both the nature of sexual violence and gendered social relations. It is possible to read these young women's explanations as born from either 'stupidity' or 'false consciousness': despite direct experience of interpersonal sexual violence, the focus of discussion remained fixed on strangers. However, I argue these narratives must be examined in the context of a media which bombards young women and men with images of the stranger rapist. This image is reinforced by parents, family and schools who support the notion that girls and women experience violence from strangers rather than friends and family.

Moreover, it is clear from the previous narratives and the ones that follow that whilst males are assumed to have responsibility for initiating sexual relations, females remain responsible for limiting these same sexual relations. Young women are keenly aware that they are likely to be held responsible for their own victimization and within this context, the focus on stranger rape becomes clear. Girls and women are less likely to be blamed for stranger rape than they are for acquaintance, date or partner rape and it is less threatening to focus attention on that which is viewed as 'out of their hands' rather than what females are supposed to be able to control.[4]

*The Making of Meaning: Explaining Sexual Violence through Gender
Difference*

I was keenly interested in how female and male adolescents understood
their experiences of dating violence, and what discourses facilitated the
negotiation of their experiences. As such, I have purposefully focused the
analysis on the various discourses sustained by these adolescents' attempts
to negotiate interpersonal heterosexual relationships. A discourse of
'biological essentialism' consistently dominated all explanations of
sexuality. Biological essentialism most powerfully establishes the meaning
of gender through 'inherent' sexual difference. The creation of gender
difference through discourse was most strongly apparent in the narratives
on sexual violence. Throughout the discussions, the implicit assumption
made was that all males 'want' sex. These adolescents quite consistently
talked about the importance of communication between women and men in
intimate situations. Men were considered obliged to obtain some sort of
consent for sex from young women. However, exactly *how* young men
obtain consent and what counts as consent raised two important issues.
First, there was an inherent contradiction between the idea of sex as
spontaneous and sex in which explicit consent must be obtained. Young
women and young men talked about their desire to have sex in which
passion and desire 'overtook' them. Talking about consent was viewed as
'spoiling the mood'. To make explicit a sexual contract, in actual sexual
relations, was not something that the young men or women actually wanted
to do.

      The second issue that discussions of consent raised was that men were
responsible for initiating sex and women were responsible for limiting
sexual relations. In all of the discussions of rape, the burden of
responsibility rested with females. Female responsibility extended to many
aspects of social relations between young men and young women. From
clothing to flirting, the association was consistently made between women
and responsibility for limiting sexual contact. My talk with Mike reflected
similar discussions in other groups:

| Myra | How do you think it sometimes comes about that guys sometimes rape women that they know or that they live with? |
| Mike | I can only see it as some sort of misunderstanding. Where the guy has been led on and he just thinks oh you've taken it this far and now you are just going to shut me out and he feels annoyed. |

Mike talks about rape as a 'misunderstanding'. He also used what became a
very familiar term in the discussions: 'led on'. The young men in this study

reported that females are responsible for both stimulating and satisfying men's sexual urges. Not surprisingly, this belief is often cited as a justification of rape. In my study, young women, through a variety of behaviors, were seen to lead men on, to promise sexual intercourse through action and then renege on that promise. The problem of logic is clear. Men are viewed as initiating sex because men are assumed to be more interested in having sex than women. But women are assumed to lead men on which implies that women are also interested in sex (at least to a certain degree). When I asked the adolescents why women lead young men on, a common answer was that women enjoy the power and control that successful leading on implies. As Joal said 'women have power over men. Men have strength but women have their bodies'. This narrative provides an explanation for women's interest in sexual activity, whilst *still* denying female sexual desire!

The mechanism through which women 'lead men on' (read, have power and control over men) seems to be the intentional use of 'mixed signals'. The boundaries of mixed signals were vague and seemed to depend more on how the man interpreted a woman's behavior than what her intentions were. Two good examples of mixed signals were clothing and substance use (whether alcohol or drugs). Most young women and men talked about the importance of women's clothing in signaling to men regarding sexual availability.[5] In the case of young men drinking, this seemed to diminish their perceived responsibility for their actions. As Mike said:

> I think the fact that he is drunk and he is really not in control of what he is doing...It's a step up from normal rape. I mean she's led him on with the added problem [sic] with the fact that he does have less control over himself.

On the other hand, the use of drugs or alcohol by a woman seemed to increase her responsibility. Women were expected to be very careful when drinking at parties in order that they not do 'anything stupid'. Young women talked about watching out for each other at parties, so that if one young woman became drunk, her young woman friends would make sure that 'nothing happened to her'. One young man described his interpretation of the effect of alcohol on sexual desire:

> If there are no words said and they are both pissed then there is no way you can pin it down to one person. Because when you are pissed, I mean alcohol provoketh [sic] desire doesn't it?

It seems that when women drink they become more responsible for themselves just as men become less responsible when they drink.

*Invoking Biology to Sustain Gender Difference and Excuse Male Violence*

Discussions with these adolescents revealed the employment of a language of gender difference to create and maintain a particular understanding of violence. This language of gender difference was accessed through socio-biological discourses. Recall the discussion of multiple gender theories which argues that the essence of a meaning is established and maintained through difference. What is male comes to be defined as everything that is not female. It was during discussions focused on sex and sexuality that assumptions of biological determination were most obvious. Biology was most often referred to in discussions of sex and sexuality. Almost all of the boys and girls assumed that males have a 'stronger sex drive' than females. As Mark explained:

> I think guys want it more than girls. Girls don't seem to be driven by their hormones half as much as guys. So guys are doing it for that reason. As far as I know guys aren't doing it as much out of peer pressure. But girls are just doing it out of being asked to do it. They don't have the drive to do it [sexual intercourse].

Mark's assumptions about male and female sexuality were shared by most of the other adolescents. I talked with Chris about male physical 'domination':

> Myra    In what ways do you think that guys are more physically dominant?
>
> Chris    It is latent but guys have the potential to be so much in control. When it all comes down to it the guy can take control and just do what he wants.

Tom used 'chemistry' to explain his attraction to a girl in his school:

> Like I liked a girl for six or seven years and I didn't really know her. It was just that the chemistry was so strong. And if a girl can wind a guy up that much in a really concentrated short period of time it is difficult to say what's going to happen. It's sometimes difficult for me to see and I don't think women can see it at all the kind of feelings it's like.

Martha even described male's sex drive as 'unconscious':

Well he feels frustrated when she keeps stopping him so he obviously thinks well she's not going to stop me this time. In some situations it is unconsciously done. I mean if it is done more consciously then it will be more forceful and more likely to be rape and then it becomes difficult to prove as to whether it was conscious or unconscious.

This understanding of the male sex drive as something 'beyond the control' of males was echoed by many of the boys:

| | |
|---|---|
| Myra | So why do some men rape? |
| Joal | Too much sexual drive. |
| Tim | They just can't read the signs. No matter what the woman does. Their need for sex is more important than... |

The narratives highlight a number of inter-related myths about male and female sexuality which critically impact on the issue of consent. These myths are sustained by a binary notion of gender which polarizes and opposes men and women. The myths include the idea that male sexuality is active as opposed to a female sexuality which is passive. Moreover, an integral part of male sexual activeness is aggression: males are assumed to be naturally sexually aggressive whilst females are naturally sexually passive. Another element of male active sexuality is their presumed knowledge about what constitutes female sexuality, or what women 'want'. Finally, the inclusion of 'hysteria' as part of femininity forefronts the idea that women do not know what they want sexually and say 'no' when they mean 'yes'. In short, if masculinity is rationality, assurance, conviction and stability, then femininity must necessarily be emotion, fickleness and indecision. A connection is then made between female artifacts, including clothes, makeup, height of shoe heel etc., and the intentional production of sexual signaling. When this perceived signaling is not accompanied by consent to have sex, the perception is that the signals were 'mixed'.

These narratives thus suggest these adolescents explain adolescent dating violence generally through this notion of difference. The main theme of this discourse consisted of understanding young men's violence towards women by way of differentiation between males and females. Talk about biological differences concentrated on vague notions of hormonal differences, differences in physical strength, differences in desire for sexual intercourse and differences in ability to control behavior. Discussions of physical violence and sexual violence most often brought out discourse based on assumptions of biological difference. The link with biology was sometimes made explicit:

I mean if we all came from a society of being all animals or whatever or living in that sort of time. If you look at the animal kingdom then the male species is more dominant.

Reeta, and other adolescents, conceived of 'the past' as a largely gendered society in which males 'dominated' females physically. First, the past was viewed in unitary terms, as though there was a single society or at least as though in all societies males dominated in exactly the same way. Second, it is the domination of *all* males over *all* females. Domination and power were conflated in a simple equation of absolute male control. The most salient feature of this argument is the conception that male domination is both inevitable and unchangeable. Related to evolutionary arguments were discussions focused on hormonal differences. As Paul said 'I think guys are driven by their hormones more than girls are'. Whilst hormones were often brought up in talk about sex, the 'hormonal argument' was certainly not restricted to issues about sex and sexuality. Hormones were also associated with male aggression as Emma described:

I was reading New Scientist and they were looking at who was most likely to be a football hooligan. And what they found out was that a lot of football hooligans are small blokes. And they went on this long spiel about the genes that cause you to be short may also be linked with the genes that cause football hooliganism.

Hormones (or genes) were assumed to dictate male's greater physical strength than female's. Differences in strength were generally assumed to emerge during early adolescence, as at least two girls in the focus groups recalled a time period in their childhood's when they were stronger than boys. So greater physical strength was not limited to the adult population, nor was it talked of in terms of individual variation. The overwhelming majority of talk in the girls' and boys' groups described boys and men as uniformly stronger than girls and women (respectively). Hormones were even employed at times to explain differences in levels of certain feelings in males and females. For instance, Rose explicitly linked hormonal differences between females and males to the emotions anger and confidence. This girl talked about boys as more angry and confident because they are 'more physically powerful' than girls. This physical power emanated from hormones. As with discussions of evolution, reference to hormones was usually vague. Some girls and boys referred specifically to testosterone as the source of all the differences. However, for most of the adolescents it seemed enough to make vague reference to 'biology' or 'hormones'. The *mechanism* of biology or hormones was never discussed.

That is, how a society based on male control emerged from a hormone and how individual boys and girls demonstrate varying levels of aggression, was left unanswered.

Male sexual need is understood to be so strong as to over-ride what a girlfriend wants and leads to an interpretation of her protests as an impediment to be overcome. Such a construction of male sexuality excuses rape, attributing responsibility to biology rather than any 'conscious' decision. Abdication of responsibility for rape was also evident in girls' stories about their own experiences of sexual coercion. Recall Rose's attempt to negotiate her experience of sexual coercion with her first boyfriend in which she tries to tell the story from both her own perspective and that of her boyfriend. She acknowledges 'there were quite a few times he forced me' but a physical reason is suggested in that 'like he blacked out or something'. The notion of misinterpretation threads through Rose's story as well; she 'went to him just for a cuddle', 'but he got the wrong impression'.

## The Absence of Female Sexuality

The narratives concerning female sexuality strongly suggested that a double standard of 'appropriate' sexuality operated for the girls. Girls were particularly expected to limit their own pleasure and desire, producing narratives replete with ambivalence towards sexuality. Girls receive conflicting messages about themselves as sexual beings. On the one hand they are barraged through popular media with the idea that they ought to be having sex but risk being labeled a 'slut' if they do become sexually active. Girls and boys' groups uniformly talked about this dichotomy, particularly the sexual double standard that encouraged boys to be sexual but disapproved of girls engaging in multiple sexual relationships. Such positioning places girls in a no-win situation. They can deny their sexuality in order to conform to expectations of 'angelic purity'. Alternatively they can allow themselves to be sexual and risk being labelled as a 'slut'. Consistent with the 'angel' identity, girls are the gatekeepers of male sexuality (Bateman, 1990). He initiates the sexual moves and she defines how far he can go. Her sexuality is a reactive one, defined by his needs rather than hers. Consistent with this notion, Fine (1988) refers to the 'silencing' of girls' sexual desire.

The dichotomised construction of female sexuality as 'slut' or 'angel' creates conflict for girls as they negotiate their sexual identities. As 'sluts', girls are expected to sexually excite boyfriends, but as 'angels' they are expected to apply the brakes to rampant male sexual desire. In this study, the boys reported that girls are responsible for both stimulating and satisfying men's sexual urges. Not surprisingly, this belief is often cited as a justification for rape. For many of the girls in the study constant pressure to engage in sexual activity wearied them into submission. Having released themselves from the position of 'angel', however, girls commonly reported feeling like 'sluts' after submitting to sex that they had not wanted.

Heteronormative sexual relations present an either/or submission to the coercion and 'prove' their love or resistance and possible loss of a boyfriend with all the emotional upheaval that such a separation may bring. Girls' talk echoed the romantic discourse in which women's priority is to maintain relationships, whilst men's priority is to maintain their own autonomy (Wetherell 1996). While the fusion of love and sex emerged as a strong theme in relation to sexual coercion, some girls suggested a dichotomized sexuality, driven by their own needs on the one hand, and romance on the other. Hence the girls in this study differentiated sexual intercourse 'for its own sake' and sexual intercourse for 'love'. Here a distinction is made between 'sex' and 'making love', the former being about need or fun, but the latter being 'special'. Sex for fun or need aligns with the 'slut' position, whilst special 'making love' anchors the position of 'angel'. 'Special sex' borrows from a romantic discourse in which 'women are supposed to do romance in relationships and men are supposed to do the sex' (Wetherell, 1995: 133). Certainly boys and girls in most groups positioned girls as desiring romance in a relationship.

Thus, sexuality presents a myriad of conflicts and dilemmas for girls. Construction of the 'good girl/bad girl' dichotomy mitigates against control of their own sexuality. Indeed the girls' accounts suggest a system of gender relations largely dominated by male need and initiation. The cost of acquiescence is high, pushing a girl from virginal 'gatekeeper' to violated 'whore'. Although girls did construct a sexuality suggestive of their own needs, there was again a dichotomous split between sex for fun on the one hand and sex as special love making on the other.

## Investment and the Will to Violence

The narratives suggest that adolescents continually practice gender. A great deal of time and energy went into clothing choice, makeup, hairstyles, comparing body sizes, and more generally *acting* in gender-appropriate ways. Moreover, this practice was informed by gender difference. It is possible to discern not only a making of gender difference, but also a relatively stable system of hierarchically positioned masculinities and femininities. This hierarchy was determined by popularity (amongst adolescents) in different contexts and the individual who was popular in a greater number of contexts was more likely to appear at the apex of the gendered hierarchy. So, for instance, a young man at the top of the masculinity hierarchy might be captain of the football team, perform well in school, be perceived as good looking and have a popular girlfriend. Both the male and female groups talked a great deal about which students were popular and unpopular in the school and what criteria was used to determine popularity. At the bottom of each hierarchy were always those practices of non-heterosexual gender. The name-calling of boys, in particular, revealed the importance placed on heterosexuality in adolescence. More favored masculine characteristics included intelligence, physical strength, sexual experience, a sense of humor and the appearance of rational control. For the young women, generally, the feminine qualities which appeared at the apex of the hierarchy were physical attractiveness, intelligence and the proven ability to maintain a relationship with a young man. For both females and males, demonstrating the ability to have intimate relationships was one of the major hallmarks of appropriate gender identity practice. A major part of masculine identity, with regard to interpersonal relationships, was the appearance of control:

| | |
|---|---|
| David | Men have images to live up to. |
| Tim | It's like blokes saying your woman should be under your thumb and everyone says this is how you should be. |
| David | I bet not one of us could say that we haven't said "you are under her thumb" to at least one of your mates. |
| Tim | Yeah. |
| David | I even said it to Paul last night. I said "you got something on your head" and he said "what is it?" and I said "it's a finger print". But when I said it he knows it's a joke. |
| Tim | Like in public if someone says "you are under the thumb" then you think "bastard" and you don't want to be seen as that and you try saying something like "oy, bitch come here" just so that... |
| Myra | But isn't a guy more likely to turn it around and say "yeah, well at least I am getting regular sex"? |
| Both | Yeah. |
| Myra | But women don't do that. Like if someone said to me that I was under a man's thumb I wouldn't say "yeah, well at least I am getting regular sex". |
| Tim | But that's what everybody sees men as. |

| David | Guys do say that. But then the next guy says "yeah, but it's with the same girl every time". And it just gets into a silly argument. |
| Arnold | I think it comes from the fact that men want to keep their relationship with their girlfriend more exclusive. They want it to be separate. Women tend to want to share it. |
| David | Yeah, I think that's true. |

Many of the young women recognized the importance of this appearance of control for young men:

| Krista | Like it took a while for him (boyfriend) to sort of be seen out with me and accept that he actually had a girlfriend rather than sort of being a lad that sort of slept around with everyone and didn't care about the woman because she was under his thumb even though I'm still under his thumb it took quite...but now...like a lot of boys don't want to be tied down to one woman even though they are madly in love. They have this image to live up to. Like "I told her". |
| Myra | How do you mean "I told her"? |
| Krista | Well, you know. "She's nagging me so I told her to piss off" or whatever. Like "she doesn't tell me what to do". Cause they have to be masculine. A lot of them are old fashioned. Like he won't ever let me see any other males. It doesn't worry me that much. |

Both the young women and men recognized the pressure to operate within the hierarchically structured gendered subject positions. The tension for the boys, in their experience of their everyday lives was palpable:

| Tim | When people say that men aren't as open as women, believe me they would be if they had the chance. |
| Myra | Do you think that is one of the reasons that men are attracted to hanging out with women just as friends, because they do get the opportunity... |
| David | I was just going to say that. It is much better if you have got half of your mates as guys and got a few girl friends who are just good friends. I feel I could talk to a girl more easily. When you talk to guys it all has to be when you are drunk. |
| Tim | Yeah. |
| David | Like you are falling down drunk with your mate and they say they love you and "don't leave me". |
| Myra | Do you think that women look at this and feel sort of superior? |
| Tim | But that's not our fault. |
| David | Men have images to live up to. |

In another group I questioned the boys about a stereotype that they had identified:

| Myra | So why don't guys want to have long-term relationships? |
| Joal | I think they do. I think it's what people are told they are allowed to think. |
| Myra | So you are saying that for a guy to say "oh I think I am in love with this person and I hope we last forever" and that kind of thing is not cool? |
| Joal | Yes. |
| Adam | I wouldn't say it. I would say it so some people, but I wouldn't say it to everyone. I mean it is so difficult. You have to watch out when you live in a society where there are so many different people where if you want to keep your self-respect, you either keep it to yourself or you only tell it to people who are not going to misunderstand it. I mean I have been crucified for saying what I think to everyone and then I just realised that you don't say that and I don't have a problem with that. I'll switch between groups of people. I mean I am not acting. I will talk about some aspects of myself and you talk about other things. You have to. It's the only way you survive. And if you don't want to get hassle and it's not worth it. You don't walk into a bunch of really hard guys and say "oh I am really in love". |

These excerpts suggest that the young men and women negotiated between a limited variety of context-dependent and contradictory subject positions and they struggle to manage these contradictory discourses. It is also clear that maintaining a discourse of hegemonic masculinity ('really hard guys') is not entirely rewarding. The narratives also suggest that these adolescents operated within a system of gendered social relations in which masculinities are hierarchically positioned above femininities (Connell, 1995). This is not to say that all men have power over all women: rather that the construction of masculinity is predicated on *assumed* superiority of men over women.

This construction of masculinity around the control of women connects the idea of investment in particular subject positions to adolescents' understanding of gender difference and the perceived utilitarianism of violence. The previous discussion supports the argument that these adolescents conceptualized gender as biologically derived and articulated mainly by difference. Added to this assumption was a perception that violence served a utilitarian function in relationships. Indeed, male violence towards girlfriends was most often described in positive, instrumental terms as a means to an end. The 'end' was sustaining the relationship:

> ...if the stress is that sometimes he doesn't know how to get through to her then I think then yes like this is the way to get through to her.

Males were particularly seen as acting reasonably if they hit their girlfriends if the female was *hysterical*. Talk of hysteria was by no means restricted to the boys groups. Girls were as likely to spontaneously provide hysteria as a reason for hitting a girl:

| Myra | Are there any situations you can think of a boy slapping his girlfriend's face? |
| Gill | No. Well, unless she was being quite hysterical. |
| Cathy | In a way I quite approve of that one because he is doing it to help her. He doesn't want her to be hysterical so he wants her to stop. It's not because he's trying to hurt her because he's angry with her. It's because he doesn't want her to be hysterical so I rather approve of it. |

In every group, 'hysteria' was defined as a female characteristic. My discussion with Jeff was typical of the adolescents' responses. Even when he refers to 'people', Jeff is actually referring exclusively to females:

| Myra | Okay. So can you imagine any situations in which it would be appropriate? |
| Jeff | I mean I think people can sometimes get quite hysterical and a slap sort of snaps you out of it. I suppose that's a rational was of thinking about it. |
| Myra | Could you imagine yourself getting hysterical and your girlfriend slapping you? |
| Jeff | I could imagine my girlfriend but I don't think I would. |
| Myra | Interesting, when I ask about this in the other groups and they say the same as you. Do you notice that "hysteria" is always linked to females? |
| Jeff | I suppose women getting hysterical is related to women screeching...because women are much more emotional. |

In the young women's group in particular, talk focused on ways of acting around boyfriends that would not irritate them *because boyfriends would be more likely to end relationships*. That is, many girls talked about the necessity of not *showing* insecurity towards boys, as boys would interpret this insecurity as curtailing their 'freedom'. Most girls accepted the fact that they were insecure about their relationships with their boyfriends: this seemed very reasonable and not worth discussing. But males were seen to control relationships in that they had the ultimate power to end the relationship. Male violence in itself was not sufficient cause for young women to end the relationship precisely because male violence was often seen in instrumental terms.

We might usefully recall here Kappeler's (1995) understanding of interpersonal relationships in terms of the exchange of commodities. Adolescence may be viewed as a period in which individuals begin to engage in a lengthy process of the negotiation of interpersonal relationships. Adolescents may either become intimately involved in several relationships within a short period of time or sustain the same relationship over a number of years. Adolescents will have, by this time, observed a variety of interpersonal relationships such as those of adults, older siblings and friends and adolescents bring these observations and expectations to their new relationships. Adolescents who 'date' and 'go steady' are investing in an established system of intimate relationships based on commodification in which each partner invests, to a greater or lesser extent, with a concomitant set of expectations. These expectations are produced by a belief in 'rights' that underlies the system of relationship commodification itself. It is possible to theorize that adolescent interpersonal violence is the behavioral action of adolescents who invest in subject positions that require the maintenance of control and mastery in interpersonal relationships. Discourses of gender difference provide an important foundation for heterosexual interpersonal violence. Biological theories of difference encourage individuals to think that they are naturally *predetermined* to be different from their partners and that their partners will be *naturally* (read, unavoidably) different from their own. Biological theories allow heterosexual males to assume that their female partners will be emotional and sometimes hysterical. These same theories allow heterosexual women to assume that their male partners will be naturally aggressive and have a 'natural' need to control. Indeed, part of sustaining a relationship with a man will be predicated on a woman's ability to manage her partner's control of her through the self-surveillance of her own behavior. And, indeed, the narratives suggest that masculine subject positions are generally founded on the ability to control women.

## Notes

1    'First sex' was defined by the young men in this study as the penetration of the man's penis into the woman's vagina until climax was achieved.

2    Several programs have developed to address adolescent dating violence. In Massachusetts, Emerge (a program that counsels men who batter) and Transition House (a shelter for battered women) joined forces to create the Dating Violence Intervention Project (Sousa, 1991). The program includes workshops, assembly talks, in-service training for school staff, an information table at Parent Night and theatre presentations of improvised dating violence scenes. The Centre for Battered Women in Austin, Texas runs a Teen Dating Violence Project in a number of middle and high schools. Similarly, the Battered Women's Alternatives in Concord, California manages a Teen Program (Levy, 1991). Both of these programs work with teenagers who are either in abusive relationships, the daughters of battered women or survivors of long-term family violence. Through a series of retreats and discussion groups teenage young women learn how to define violence, the dynamics of violent relationships and alternatives to abuse. Similarly, Ginny NiCarthy and Ann Muenchow created a program in Seattle, Washington (NiCarthy, 1991). Working in two schools, NiCarthy and Muenchow put together a creative nine-part program dealing with addictive love and abuse. This goal of this program was to define addictive love and explore its relationship to abuse in teenage relationships. I directed a Violence Prevention Project in Montreal, Canada between 1991 and 1992 (see Bula, 1992). The goal of this project was to highlight the problem of adolescent violence and suggest viable alternatives to violence.

3    The bulk of my data came from seventeen single-gender discussion groups that students from two schools participated in for about a year. I tape-recorded all of the group discussions and analyzed the transcripts of these discussions. I have changed all the names of the young women and I quote in order to protect their anonymity. In the quoted text, I referred to my own talk as 'Myra'.

4    This is not to imply that girls and women are not blamed and made responsible for stranger rape. However, I am suggesting that in cases of interpersonal sexual violence the female's behavior becomes even more scrutinized.

5    All the adolescents who talked about clothing reported that it should not matter what a young woman wore, but that 'in the real world' what a young woman wore affected how she was perceived and, more importantly, how likely she would be held responsible for her own victimization. Interestingly, several young women defended their own choice of clothing, often saying that they wore what was 'comfortable' or 'fashionable'. Young women are left to negotiate a very complex set of guidelines that are often contradictory. If they dress the way popular magazines tell them they should, they risk being labeled 'sluts'. If they dress in such a way as to avoid being blamed for being sexually violated, young women will certainly win no fashion or popularity contests. Moreover, many young women would argue that, in *both* cases, they are dressing to please an outside 'judge' rather than themselves. Many young women told me that they felt they should be able to dress however they want *and* be free from violence.

# Chapter 5

# Investing in Masculinity: Men Who Use Interpersonal Violence

Chapter Three argued that in attempting to negotiate a very complex social environment, young children quickly learn to identify gender as a salient marker of difference by which they can, and indeed are expected, to 'order' their world. Male children, particularly, learn that aggression and violence are key markers of their gender. Chapter Four drew on this argument to suggest how adolescents negotiate societal expectations of heteronormativity. The narratives provided reveal an invocation of socio-biological discourses to produce accentuated gender differences which in turn provide the rationalization for the use of aggressive and violent tactics. That is, particular discourses, especially those which emphasize gender differences, sustain young men's use of violence as an effective and sometimes 'necessary' means of meeting their sexual needs from young women who are positioned as 'other'. In the present chapter, I want to further this argument by suggesting that hegemonic heterosexual masculinity is centrally organized around aggression and the willingness to practice violence. This hegemonic masculinity is constantly under challenge, as other practices of masculinity and femininity call into question, and potentially undermine the conditions under which masculinity is founded. Heterosexual interpersonal violence, then, becomes the outcome of discourses which position females as effectively a different species incapable of communicating in the same way as men. But violence is also the outcome of the threat to the investment in hegemonic heterosexual masculinities predicated on the superiority of men over women. This chapter will particularly focus on the structure of modern heterosexual intimate relationships, which I will argue provides a context most conducive to the practice of violence.

The personal safety measures women are advised to practice reveal an underlying assumption that women need to protect themselves from strangers. Consequently, women who live with their partners are assumed to be in *less* danger in their homes than single women, despite the fact that women are most likely to be attacked by their (ex)husbands or (ex)partners. Assault within intimate relationships has reached epidemic proportions. The National Clearinghouse of the Defense of Battered Women estimates a domestic assault is reported every fifteen seconds (Moseley-Braun, 1993). Between three and five million women are beaten every year. Surgeon General Antonia Novella claims that domestic violence causes more injuries to women than the collective injuries sustained from rapes, muggings and car accidents (Spaid, 1993). The assault of women by their husbands or lovers is the second highest form of serious injury (after male to male assault). The Federal Bureau of Investigation reports that wife battering is the most underreported crime in America. Pregnancy statistically increases the likelihood that a woman will be battered by her partner. The United States March of Dimes concludes that birth defects directly caused by battering affect more babies than all the diseases combined to which children are normally immunized against (Gibbs, 1993).

As many as one in three women will be sexually assaulted in their lifetimes. In the United States, it is estimated that a woman is raped every five minutes (Feinstein, 1993). Women in the United States have a twenty to thirty percent chance of being raped or experience attempted rape. Some researchers estimate the chances of a woman being raped in her lifetime are closer to forty percent. In Britain, self-report surveys recorded a seventeen percent incidence rate for rape and a twenty percent incidence rate for attempted rape. Canadian statistics provide a similarly bleak picture. In 1994, there were a total of 31,690 sexual assaults reported to the police. The majority of these assault, 31,560 were sexual assaults, 768 involved a weapon and 362 were aggravated sexual assaults. In Australia, the police recorded 12,809 victims of sexual assault. For every 100,000 people, there were 71 sexual assault victims (Australian Bureau of Statistics, 1995). The vast majority (over eighty percent) of these victims were females. Whilst sexual offences make up less than one percent of all crime in New Zealand, the total number of sexual offences has increased between 1986 and 1995 from 3,200 to 4,378 (Statistics New Zealand, 1996). During this nine-year period, the rate of sexual attacks has increased by a startling ninety-seven percent, from 1,517 to 2,993. Within the category of 'sexual attacks' sexual violation offences have increased by one hundred and twenty-seven percent, from 508 in 1986 to 1,155 in 1995. Other forms of sexual attack have increased by eighty-two percent, from 1,009 to 1,838 in the past nine years.

**Physical and Psychological Violence**

Men who violently attack their (ex)partners are often portrayed by the media as mentally disturbed, abnormal and constituent of a small minority of the male population. Films such as *Silence of the Lambs* and *Seven* reinforce the image that violent men are psychotic, friendless and live on the margins of society whilst assaulting unknown victims. Headlines such as, 'woman under protection was raped by stalker' (Guardian, 1996: 2) portray the 'stalker' as psychologically disturbed. The conclusion that current rates of personal violence most likely underestimate the actual amount of interpersonal violence is important because it essentially refutes the 'marginal act' theory of interpersonal violence. Moreover, research can uncover no consistent differences between men who commit interpersonal violence the normal male population (Groth and Brinbaum, 1979).

The commonly held belief that men who assault women are somehow 'abnormal', rests in large part on how interpersonal violence is defined. In *Why Men Hate Women* Adam Jukes contends that a more accurate and inclusive definition of psychological, physical and sexual forms of interpersonal violence should include:

- slap, punch, grab, kick, choke, push, restrain, pull hair, pinch, bite, rape, use force, threats or coercion to obtain sex or indulge in sexual practices which she does not want.
- use of weapons, throwing things, keeping weapons around which frighten her.
- abuse of furniture, pets, destroying her possessions, tearing or spoiling her clothing.
- intimidation - standing in the doorway during arguments, angry or threatening gestures, use of your size to intimidate, standing over her, driving recklessly, uninvited touching, covering her mouth to stop her talking.
- threats of violence, verbal or non-verbal, direct or indirect, self-inflicted injury - for example, hitting your head on walls or threatening suicide.
- harassment - for example, uninvited visits or calls, following her, checking up on her, not leaving when asked.
- isolation, preventing or making it hard for her to see or talk to friends, relatives and others. Making derogatory comments about her friends.
- yelling, swearing, being coarse, raising your voice, using angry expressions or gestures, embarrassing her.

- criticism, name-calling, swearing, mocking, put-downs, ridicule, accusations, blaming humiliating. Angrily waking her up from sleep.
- pressure tactics - pushing her to make decisions or hurry up, walking in front of her, using guilt, sulking, threats of withholding financial support, manipulating the children.
- interrupting, changing the subject, not listening or responding, picking up the newspaper when she wants to talk, twisting her words, topic-stringing.
- economic harassment - getting angry with her about 'where the money goes', not allowing access to money, the car or other resources, sabotaging her attempts to work, believing you are the provider and thinking that she could not survive without you, saying that the money you earn is yours.
- claiming the truth, being the authority. Claiming the right to define what is logical, rational, reasonable or fair in the relationship. Calling her stupid or otherwise defining her behavior as illogical, unreasonable, irrational, etc. Logic-chopping, lying, withholding information about your activities, infidelity.
- using pornography, including home videos, against her wishes.
- not helping with child-care or housework, saying that you have already done a day's work. Not keeping to agreements. Abusing your power over the children, either emotionally or physically.
- feeling stressed and tense, and using this to get into a frame of mind where you blame her for everything which goes wrong: things you can't find, mess, etc.
- emotional withholding - not expressing your feelings or giving support, thinking your problems are more important than hers, not giving attention or compliments, not respecting her feelings, rights or opinions. Not initiating conversation about the relationship, but expecting that your partner will do it all. Sulking.
- not taking care of yourself and refusing to learn basic life skills, cooking, etc. Abusing drugs, alcohol, not eating properly, not making friends and seeking help and support from them. Believing you have the right to define appropriate wifely and motherly behavior, and not offering your expectations to negotiation. Criticizing her motherly qualities or performance. Accusing her of neglecting the children or using threats of taking them away, etc.
- telling her that if she doesn't like it she knows what she can do - pack, leave, etc. Not acknowledging that the relationship is important to you, telling her that you don't need her or love her, etc. (1993: 295-296).

The inclusion of even a fraction of these forms of abuse, results in much higher numbers of people who would be defined as violent towards their (ex)partners.[1] We do not tend to include such an exhaustive list when contemplating what constitutes physical and psychological violence. Although this point will be discussed later, I want to suggest here that interpersonal relationships are largely configured in terms of a particular kind of commodity exchange involving nebulous, transient and elusive things such as love, trust, care, commitment, joy and attention. Interpersonal relationships are 'supposed' to include anything *but* control, manipulation and violence. This means that in the context of interpersonal relationships, acts of violence are less likely to be acknowledged than the same acts committed by strangers, because these actions contradict our everyday assumptions and beliefs about the 'nature' of intimacy.

**Sexual Violence**

It is estimated that between fourteen percent and twenty-five percent of women are raped by their husbands at least once during their marriages (Resnick et al., 1991; Russell, 1982, 1990). Marital rape and adolescent date rape may be the most common forms of rape in society (Jenny, 1988; Kennedy Bergen, 1995). Moreover, research on marital rape refutes any notion that this is a relatively harmless act. In a study of fifty survivors of marital rape, Kennedy Bergen (1995) identified three forms of rape including 'force-only rapes' characterized by the use of enough physical force to ensure sexual intercourse:

> He shoved me down on the bed very forcefully and I said, "What are you doing? ...No, I don't want this". And there was no preliminaries and no tenderness. Nothing. And he entered me and it was painful and I just remember being so repulsed (p.120).

The most common form of marital rape was categorized as 'battering rape' which involved beatings combined with forced sex:

> He would fight me and then he would always rip all of my clothes off me. I don't have hardly any clothes left because he always ripped off my clothes and I was naked. Then he would try to lay on me and put it in. Sometimes I was able to fight him off and I would fight like wild and he wouldn't be able to get it in. But usually he would [succeed in penetrating her] and he put me

in the hospital a lot. He broke my nose, and my jaw and cut my wrists. (p.121).

'Obsessive rapes' were characterized by rape combined with 'strange and perverse' acts:

> He was really into watching porno movies and he tried to make me do all sorts of things. And I don't like it. He hurt my stomach so bad because I was pregnant and he was making me do these things. I think he's a sadist - he pulls my hair and punches me and slaps me and makes me pass out. (p.121-122).

Many women experience a combination of these forms of rape throughout the course of their relationships. The women in this study underwent a complex process of redefining the sexual violence they experienced as 'rape'.[2] The struggle these women experienced in defining what happened to them reflects a societal reluctance to define forced sex between intimate partners as 'rape'. One survivor of wife rape recalled:

> There was no such thing as marital rape. People didn't even talk about regular [stranger] rape. And there certainly weren't any shelters. It was a personal problem (p.130).

Similarly, another woman reported:

> ...He raped me - he ripped off my pajamas, he beat me up. I mean some scumbag (sic) down the street would do that to me. So to me it wasn't any different because I was married to him, it was rape...It emotionally hurt worse [than stranger rape]. I mean you can compartmentalize it as stranger rape - you were at the wrong place at the wrong time - you can manage to get over it differently. But here you're at home with your husband and you don't expect that. I was under constant terror [from then on] even if he didn't do it (p. 132).

The lack of available discourse to identify sexual violence committed by partners concurs with the discussion of sexual violence within adolescent dating relationships discussed in the previous chapter. Moreover, marital rape convictions are difficult because trials primarily consist of the competing testimonies of wife and husband. It is not just that men's voices are usually valued over women's: the association between heterosexual sex and violence also plays a major role in denying the realities of women who are raped by their male partners. This point will be taken up in the following sections.

**Theorizing Masculinity**

At the turn of the last century women's suffrage was clearly on many nation's agenda and as women slowly began to infiltrate the hallowed halls of academia and the professions, a reactive political interest in determining differences between the genders took hold. Since that time an enormous amount of research has focused on gender differences: psychological differences in attitude, behavior, emotion, reaction, parental 'instinct' and so on. The development of medical science has allowed for a corresponding search for biological differences: brain size and shape, genetic structure, physical reaction to stimuli, hormone levels etc. As Chapter Two discussed, the idea of gender roles developed during this period and has, until recently, been hardly contested. Gender roles for men invariably centered around work outside the home, assumed to be the defining feature of masculinity. Most research of this sort focused on the individual man's ability to fulfill his masculine role; the greater the assimilation, the more socially and emotionally adjusted the man was supposed to be.

Second-wave feminism called into question the appropriateness of gender roles assigned to women, and indeed, the fact that gender roles had been socially assigned in the first place. Anthropological research testified to significant variation between societies in terms of gender roles, clearly demonstrating that a variety of masculinities had, and were being practiced around the world. In some societies homosexuality was practiced by the majority of males and viewed as an integral part of normal masculine development. In other societies, men did not commit violent acts such as rape (Sanday, 1981). It was clear, then, that gender roles were both historically and culturally specific: what was considered 'normal' masculine practice in one society was considered 'abnormal' in another. The feminist movement made clear the political drive of much sex role theory: it was in men's best interests to maintain women in positions of economic dependence by keeping women from paid employment, isolated in their homes and responsible for both child and husband care. The economic, political and social subordination of half the human race was justified through the deployment of the sex role system.

In response to the feminist charge, some men began to regard masculine roles to actually be detrimental to men. Warren Farrell (1987) and others criticized men's roles, especially as a consequence of new feminist demands on men. Not only were men now expected to 'bring home the bacon'; they also had to do their fair share of the housework and child care as well as become 'sensitive' to their female partner's needs. The 'new man' had to retain the responsibilities of the traditional male sex role *and* incorporate supposedly feminine roles including caring, sharing and sensitivity. As one strand of the new men's movement set about trying to address the issues raised by the women's movement, particularly with regard to male sexism and violence, another strand focused on men's oppression and saw the women's movement as an overcompensation for women's subordination, effectively elevating the status of women beyond equality with men to a position of superiority.

What gender role theory failed to do was develop any sustained analysis of the dynamic interplay of individuals with these roles. Moreover, roles were broadly assigned according to gender, whilst scant attention was paid to differences in social class, ethnicity, race and so on. Also problematic was the assumed reciprocity between masculine and feminine roles, conceptualized as complementary and mutually exclusive. Gender role theory also defined gay men as dysfunctional, not able to assimilate to 'normal' and 'appropriate' roles. Since the 1970s, and particularly in this decade, a sustained focus on masculinity, as a subject in need of investigation in its own right (as opposed to the philosophy of 'Man') has resulted in a growing number of texts and articles concerned with the dialectic relation between masculinity and the social world.[3]

## Common Explanations of Male Violence Against Women

Two of the most frequently cited factors theorized to contribute to male violence against women are television viewing and pornography. Now that television has entered the lives of virtually all members of Western society, questions about the influence of this pervasive medium on children, in particular, have become salient.[4] Numerous books and articles have been written on the influence of television viewing on behavior. Over 235 studies have specifically investigated the correlation between television violence and violence in society (Miedzian, 1991). Two divergent arguments hypothesize the influence of television violence on male behavior. Evolutionary and psychological theories suggest that viewing violence on television may serve a 'cathartic' function by which males reduce *inherent* violence by watching violent acts on television. However, the American Psychological Association suggests a positive correlation between the aggressive behavior of Americans and their viewing of violence on television, citing an increased homicide rate from 7,942 in the 1950s to 21,860 in 1990s (Miedzian, 1991). Children who watch just two to four hours of television per day will have seen an average of 89,000 murders and 100,000 acts of violence by the time they leave elementary school (Schumer, 1992).[5] Watching violent television tends to increase antisocial and aggressive behavior for all ages levels. Comstock (1991) for instance, concluded that 'in magnitude, television violence is as strongly correlated with aggressive behavior as any other behavioral variable that has been measured'. Hypothesizing a correlation between virtual and real violence, some researchers suggest that if television had never been invented America would have, per year, 10,000 fewer homicides, 70,000 fewer rapes and 700,000 fewer assaults causing bodily harm (Durenberger, 1993). The reverse is also true: when children view altruistic behavior on television it increases their levels of constructive, pro-social behavior whilst decreasing anti-social aggressive behavior.

Slasher films, as a genre, have been the subject of controversy from their creation. In these films, women and men are terrorized, tortured, mutilated, and killed. Although not as widely viewed as mainstream adventure films, slasher films nevertheless enjoy a steady audience. It appears that slasher films are a means through which young men practice a particular masculinity characterized by the ability to force themselves to watch extreme violence without flinching or otherwise demonstrating fear. Some association between exposure to extreme violence in film and violence has also been made and some studies have found that watching slasher films increases men's tolerance for violence over time (Donnerstein et al., 1987). After seeing slasher films over several days, depictions that produced anxiety and depression earlier were later judged less violent, degrading and offensive. The men perceived female rape victims to be less injured when they had viewed several rape scenes and became less able to empathize with female rape victims.

Whilst slasher films appeal to a relatively small audience, 'adventure' films are also cause for concern. With few exceptions, the characters perform very stereotyped gendered scripts. Women are most often cast in the role of the useless 'damsel in distress', unless she is a villain too. In many films only villainous women are equated with violence. Whilst, recent films such as *Thelma and Louise* depict a wider range of femininities, these films associate female equality with violence. Women, such as Mallory in *Natural Born Killers*, become 'cool' when they act violently. The message of such films is that violence is an acceptable and appropriate means of problem-solving. Men are rarely considered 'cool' when they become less violent.

The hypothesized association between masculinity, exposure to violence on television and the commission of violent acts is also made with regard to pornography. On one side of the debate are those who contend that no clear association has been made between the use of pornography and the commission of violence.[6] Furthermore, moves towards the censuring of pornography are viewed as opposing libertarian goals of freedom of expression.[7] Strossen (1995: 248) proposes that the censorship of pornography rests on three inter-related assumptions: that exposure to sexist, violent imagery leads to sexist, violent behavior; that the effective suppression of pornography would significantly reduce exposure to sexist, violent imagery; and that censorship would effectively suppress pornography. Although several studies do show a correlation between the availability of pornography and sexual offense rates, no studies have made a causal link between pornography and the use of violence against women. Feminist anti-censorship campaigners contend that focusing on pornography diverts energy and attention away from the 'real' causes of women's inequality such as sex-segregated labor markets, the unpaid work of women and violence against women. Furthermore, legislation against pornography is believed to suggest that women are incapable of defending themselves.

On the other side of the debate are those who contend that pornography harms women, supports an unrealistic and unhealthy view of women's sexuality and contributes to the high levels of violence against women.[8] For anti-pornography campaigners, suggesting that women simply 'stand up for themselves' misses the crucial analysis of power in which sexual relations exist in society. Pornography is not simply the sum of a collection of images of women having sex. Nor do judges define arbitrarily what is considered pornographic and what is considered erotic: gender and sexuality are socially constructed. Pornography institutionalizes male supremacy through imagery, re-creating and sustaining the subordination of women. Men masturbate to a particular image of women and pornography defines the power men have over women:

> In pornography, there it is, in one place, all of the abuses that women had to struggle so long even to begin to articulate, all the unspeakable abuse: the rape, the battery, the sexual harassment, the prostitution, and the sexual abuse of children. Only in pornography it is called something else: sex, sex, sex, sex, and sex, respectively (MacKinnon, 1987, p.171).

In this way, pornography is far from radical: it is, in fact, business as usual. As MacKinnon points out '[s]how me an atrocity to women, I'll show it to you eroticized in the pornography' (MacKinnon, 1987: 151). Just as legislative and public response to partner rape can only be understood within the framework of an inherent association between heterosexual sex and violence, pornography has been defined as sexual rather than violent. Because rape and pornography are erotic to men: they *are* erotic:

> to reject forced sex in the name of women's point of view requires an account of women's experience of being violated by the same acts both sexes have learned as natural and fulfilling and erotic, since no critique, no alternatives, and few transgressions have been permitted (MacKinnon, 1987, p.161).

Pornography is certainly a means through which many boys and girls learn about female anatomy and a particular version of female sexuality (Baker, 1992). Consuming pornography is often a way for boys to show that they are entering a 'man's world'. I would certainly argue that most pornography depicts a fairly narrow and stereotypical version of human sexuality. In the first instance, almost all pornography reproduces heterosexualism. According to the pornographic argument, female sexuality is presented in terms of availability, a desire and need to be dominated by men and a preference for penile penetration. Female sexuality is most obviously and explicitly dependent upon men. Women experience arousal and orgasm from sexual practices that males find stimulating, such as oral sex and vaginal penetration. Young girls enjoy having sex with adult men. However, I think that male sexuality is no less defined by pornography: men must be capable of constant arousal, superior sexual performance and a sexual desire most stimulated by subjugated women. It may not be necessary to extend an argument beyond that of 'pornography is violence against women'. However, with regard to the male use of pornography and a direct causal link with violence against women, I am not convinced that such a thesis can be sustained. What most pornography does do is emphasize differences between women and men, reproducing an entirely scripted and predictable performance of sexuality, gender identity and gendered social interaction.

Discussion of pornography highlights concern about the meaning of heterosexuality, the limits of its possible practice, and especially the negative implications for women. As I stated earlier, how sexual violence should be defined is a contested matter. Some scholars, such as Catherine MacKinnon (1987) argue that our current separation of sexual assault from other forms of physical assault betrays men's confusion of sex with violence.[9] MacKinnon (1987) points out that the law, reflecting men's definitions, has distinguished between 'rape' on the one hand and 'sexual intercourse' on the other. The problem is that definitions of 'normal' sexual intercourse often overlap with definitions of 'rape' or sexual violation. Since criminal law is intended to punish deviant acts, in the context of 'normal' heterosexual relations, men will rarely be viewed as violent.[10]

Conceptions of 'normal' heterosexual sex and the sanctification of marriage often consequences the treatment of marital rape as a 'special case'. Marital rape has only very recently received serious scholarly and public attention, well on the heels of wife assault. The criminalizing of marital rape in the United States, Canada, England, Australia and New Zealand reveals the slow and reluctant acceptance of marital rape as a criminal offense.[11] And yet the high incidence of sexual violence within intimate relationships belies a personal relation system based around the exchange and the commodification of sexual intercourse.

## Situating Intimate Relations Within Heteronormativity

Whilst television violence and pornography have enjoyed a great deal of exposure to academic study and criticism, the dynamics of intimate relationships has often gone unattended because of its taken-for-granted status in our heteronormative society. Intimate relationships have undergone a transformation concurrent with a larger transformation from pre-industrial to modern (or postmodern) society. Beck and Beck-Gernsheim's *The Normal Chaos of Love* (1995) outlines changes to the structural institution of marriage, as well as attitudes towards the meaning of marriage. In 'premodern' society, Beck and Gernsheim suggest that interpersonal relationships were structured through a network of traditional ties, including the family business, religion, community and gender role. These structural parameters at the same time both structured and restricted individual choice. Stability, protection and a certainty of identity were exchanged for the severe restriction of individual choice. It was not simply a matter of duty: the very survival of individuals necessitated the consistent performance of roles. Each institution, from the family to the Church reinforced both the roles and counseled individuals to maintain these roles.

The family had a particularly important role in maintaining and reproducing societal functioning. The designated roles of individuals within the family varied a great deal depending on social class. One of the crucial axes on which these roles were determined was gender.[12] Industrialization, and the transition to modern society, brought about a large number of far-reaching and complex changes to structure of society and the family as well as individual attitudes, beliefs and social relationships (Beck and Beck-Gernsheim, 1995). Political restructuring from sovereign to state rule was fueled by philosophical questioning of religious faith. As both Max Weber (1985) and Emile Durkheim (1933) suggest in their related analyses, the socio-political shift from pre-industrial religious society to post-industrial secular society set individuals adrift from their traditional beliefs, resulting in growing individual isolation and increased expectation to command one's own life. Individuals gained freedom to control their own destinies, but this freedom also demanded to be taken. Capitalism ushered in an era in which the individual became responsible for her or his economic survival. Michael Moore's classic film *Roger and Me* graphically illustrates the devastation wreaked on American General Motors worker's lives when, at the same time that record profits were made by this company, 'downsizing' led to mass unemployment. Rather than assume any responsibility for the economic or social consequences of this sudden mass unemployment, workers were admonished to 'take control of their own lives'.

Capitalism, secularization, nuclearization of families, urbanization and increased mobility led to the 'individualizing' of society. The standard of living has increased, as have educational opportunities. This has meant a dramatic increase in the number of young people able to free themselves from struggle for daily familial survival to pursue individual interests. It has also meant the recognition of youth itself as a psycho-social stage of development in its own right. Gone are many of the restraints of traditional beliefs, customs and communities; but so are many of the benchmarks through which people derived meaning and stability. Freed from the grind of daily survival, individuals are now freer to consider other dimensions of their existence than the purely physical. This coincides with the psychologization and capitalization of individuality. As Ehrenreich and English point out:

> In the post-romantic world, where the old ties no longer bind, all that matters is you: you can be what you want to be; you choose your life, your environment, even your appearance and your emotions…The old hierarchies of protection and dependency no longer exist, there are only free contracts, freely terminated. The marketplace, which long ago expanded to include the relations of production, has now expanded to include all relationships (1979, p.276).

Interpersonal relationships are no longer accepted as overt business arrangements designed to further familial interests. Our personal identities have become keenly bound up with our abilities to develop and sustain personal relationships. Love and intimacy are no longer 'bonuses'; they are necessary features of marital and de facto relationships. Commodification has gone underground: the discourse of explicit exchange of goods and services has been replaced by a discourse of intimacy and relationships.

Personal relationships operate in the same way as do business or work relationships. Firstly, all relationships are predicated on the ideas of production and exchange: in work relationships, labor power is exchanged for pay or goods and services. In personal relationships, goods and services produced are also exchanged. These goods and services may be recognizable as exchanging money derived from work for the care of children; or they may be more subtle as in the exchange of love for trust. By working, each individual in society produces labor power, and this labor power has a particular value. In capitalist society, the value of labor is controlled by market forces which in turn is determined by the buyer of labor. In order to profit, those who buy labor power (mostly by paying their workers a wage) must receive surplus value over and above the cost of the labor power and the costs of producing the goods. Thus workers do not receive the true worth of their labor.

Shulamith Firestone (1970) and more recently, Susan Kappeler (1995) have applied Marxian precepts concerning this exchange of labor to interpersonal relationships. In her analysis, Kappeler notes the dramatic shift from the pre-industrial citizen-husband/slave-wife relationship, to an emphasis on equal partnership. The relationship itself becomes the main focus, as is the securing of a partner to form and sustain this relationship. And relationships have become one more element of economic production as individuals identify themselves as use-value producers:

> 'private' individuals conceive of themselves as the private producers of their own lives, whose partial products acquire value from the work invested and may be exchanged with similar private products. Whatever we do, every 'productive activity' of daily life, does not just remain use-value as lived experience, but becomes 'useful work' and a product of labour which acquires the fetish character of the commodity (1995, p.186).

In today's world, we produce ourselves and all of the 'products' which we freely exchange for the 'products' of others. These products still include such traditionally exchanged good and services as the home, children, the 'family wage'; as well as friendship, intimacy, closeness, trust and affection. Each individual assesses her or his own needs and desires and goes in search of a potential 'supplier of the desired goods' (p.187). Kappeler supports the conception of relationship goods and services as exchanged commodities through the accepted notion of personality as the collection of quantifiable characteristics. Thus we speak of people we know as 'selfish' or 'generous', 'funny' or 'bland'. Moreover, we calculate the costs (what we must exchange) and benefits (what we expect to receive) in the development of acquaintances, friendships and intimate partners. In public economic relationships, buying and selling occurs: in private relationships we 'give and take' (Kappeler, 1995). This common adage has particular meaning in this context: rather than demand creating a supply to satisfy it; goods are supplied in relationships which create a demand for payment. That is, we 'give' as advance payment, things which have not been requested. Once goods and services have been given, payment can then be demanded. In the modern relationships, there is supposed to be an equivalency to this exchange of goods and services, although what has been exchanged continues to be sex-specific in many cases. So men, for instance, are commonly assumed to exchange social commodities such as wages, fatherhood and stability whilst women are assumed to exchange intimacy, caring, motherhood and sex.[13] Moreover, this exchange is a complicated process. First of all, we tend to be reticent about acknowledging that any exchange is taking place at all.[14] Secondly, the terms of the exchange are rarely made explicit. Thirdly, since the individual gives things which have not been requested, the giver necessarily gambles that the receiver will take and will give in return. The receiver, on the other hand, does not get to name the price for any things received, nor, indeed, necessarily designate which individuals may 'give freely' to her/him.

Thus, relationships invoke a number of signifiers: agency, identity, emotion, sexuality, interest and power. The self-interest involved in personal relationships is evident in the terms of the exchange: we want to be loved, to be cared for, to be recognized, to be made happy. We will love, care for, recognize and make happy that individual who provides these things for us; and we will deliver these goods and services on the condition that they are returned. Power structures these exchanges. Not only are the discourses which we employ shaped by power relations, but the very exchange of goods and services itself is only possible as a power relation. That is, 'the one who succeeds in determining the price from their point of view is the one that wins and profits' (Kappeler, 1995: 201). Even when exchanges are ostensibly equivalent, the structure within which the exchanges take place involves power. Power in personal relationships is perhaps most obvious when it involves violence and it is to this aspect of relationships that I now turn.

## Theorizing Masculinity and Heterosexual Interpersonal Violence

Those familiar with the literature on violence against women will concur that a great deal of this research is devoted to theorizing *why* many women remain in violent interpersonal relationships and *how* men commit personal violence. For instance, survivors of wife battering, shelter workers and psychologists often report a 'cycle' of abuse. Lenore Walker (1984) describes a three-phase cycle consisting of a *tension building* phase during which the man becomes increasingly dissatisfied with whatever his female partner does; an *acute battering* phase during which the man attacks his partner and she is beaten, raped, verbally assaulted for a few minutes or several days; and finally a phase of *loving contrition* during which the man expresses remorse, promising never to repeat the battering. Whilst the cycle of violence theory may explicate the dynamics of abusive interpersonal relationships, it does little to explain *why* men are violent towards women they know. Likewise, attempting to theorize why women remain within violent interpersonal relationships entirely misses the problem of male volition.

Attempting to move beyond analyses of the dynamics of male violence against women towards an analysis of power, the *Power and Control Wheel* introduced by the Domestic Abuse Intervention Project illustrates the ways in which psychological, physical and sexual violence is used in interpersonal relationships (see Yllö, 1993: 55). According to this paradigm, violent men use various control tactics to gain or maintain control over their female partners, including: intimidation, emotional abuse, isolation, children, male privilege, economic abuse, coercion and threats, and minimizing, denying and blaming. Many women in violent relationships are subjected to several, or all, of these tactics. The picture that emerges from this model is a relationship based more on domination than conflict management. That is, the abuse of female partners is less a struggle between two persons of equal power and resources: male interpersonal violence in the context of an unequal gendered society is based on control, entitlement, intimidation and fear. This analysis recognizes that men stand to benefit from violence against women. Recalling the analysis of interpersonal relationships as commodity exchange systems, the violent man obtains various commodities (sexual intercourse, dinner served on time etc.) whilst also securing the more valued commodity of his partner's subjectivity. The power and control model provides a compelling argument concerned with the dynamics of male personal violence: the *how* of violence. It is possible to extend this model with the insights developed in the previous chapters to explicate the *why* of violence.

If we accept the notion that gender differences are relational rather than essential, larger differences *within* genders than *between* genders necessitates the constant re-creation of differences between females and males. This means that in order to maintain gender difference as a central organizing principle, we must somehow maintain the illusion that women and men are polar opposites in the face of lived experience and ample evidence of between-sex similarity and within-sex difference. We struggle to en-gender behavior by making our behaviors gender-specific. Behavior becomes delineated by separation and inequality. Violent men, in particular, take this goal to extremes. Male interpersonal violence thus represents:

> a man's attempt to reassert gender difference and gender dominance, when his terror of not being different enough from 'his' woman threatens to overtake him (Goldner et al., 1990, p.348).

Men who use violence against women in their interpersonal relationships choose this action because they perceive their identity, their selfhood, to be under threat. Violent men are afraid that their wives are as strong, capable and rational: in other words, as 'male' as they are. Violence expresses the terror that a man is not so different from his wife, or any female, which immediately raises suspicions that women and men generally may not be so different.

Gender is strongly connected to power and benefits are accrued to the identification with particular masculinities. As Chapter Two argued, gender practices are not equally available to every individual. Race, social class, nationality, regionality and a host of other factors makes the taking on of a more circumscribed sphere of gender identities most probable. What makes individual men choose particular masculinities is the result of a process of negotiation through which men experience greater degrees of personal pleasure and satisfaction with a particular gender practice. What pleasure is experienced will be a facet of the individual man's environment but it will also reflect a dialectic relationship between that individual and the world in which he lives. In other words, there will be overt benefits for any man to construct his gender practice in ways sanctioned and encouraged through his relations with others. Hegemonic heterosexual masculinities have been constructed and crucially defined in terms of an historical subordination of women. This subordination includes an entitlement to servicing from women: sexual, practical (cooking, shopping, cleaning), maternal (bringing up his children), emotional (supporting him through his daily life), financial and/or subservient (providing a group of individuals who will always be subservient to men). Practicing these masculinities means attempting to control women's subjectivity such that women will continue to provide this servicing. These masculinities are supported at a societal level as surveys of attitudes reflect. For instance, an Australian survey found that twenty-three percent of men believed that they were justified in shoving, kicking or hitting their female partner if she did not obey him, wasted his money, failed to keep the house clean or refused to have sexual intercourse with him (Horsfall, 1991).

The investment that individuals make in gendered identity is not the simple choice based on a rational assessment of the world and social relations. Investment in identity involves a complex process of building associations between pleasure and identifying with significant people from one's individual history. Our fantasies about who we are, how we are perceived and how we want to be perceived, our reputation and our power within social relations is powerfully linked with our choice of gendered identity (Moore, 1995). Indeed, we might view male violence against women as a measure of the falsity of gender categories (Connell, 1995). Laws may prevent women from voting, working outside the home, engaging in public life, owning property and land, or occupying certain jobs but they cannot mask the intelligence and abilities of women. No amount of violence, legal sanctions or discourse of difference has actually been able to completely silence and stifle women's ability. Women are clearly as able to perform as well as men in medicine, law, academia, the military and government. At the same time as gender discourses of difference are defined as inevitable, immutable and true, lived experience constantly stands to reveal this discourse as myth. Many men live as adults in environments in which gender difference is all that defines them as competent and autonomous and for some of these men, the maintenance of gender difference is crucial to the sustenance of this particular identity. Men who are raised in families that adhere to strict gender boundaries often face a compounded sense of the 'invasion' of women into 'man's domain'. Several studies have examined social class and income differences in domestic violence but these studies invariably focus on inter-economic differences; that is, differences between high-income and low-income families.

Fewer studies examine intra-economic differences: social class and income differences between intimate partners. Lupri's (1990) Canadian survey found that unemployed men were twice as likely to assault their wives than men in part or full-time employment. Explorations of relationships in terms of accrued differences in wealth, intelligence, abilities (to make friends, fix things, understand the world etc.) between partners would provide a fruitful means of testing multiple gender theories of the construction and continued maintenance of gender difference. Recall statistics reported earlier that women who separate from or divorce their partners are at higher risk for assault and murder by their male partners.

Leaving a male partner, whether or not she returns, expresses a very real action towards independence from that man. Men who practice masculinities predicated on gender difference and the domination of women will experience this leaving as highly threatening and as a severe loss of control.

In this sense, the problem with society is not male violence per se. It is masculinity, or more specifically, those masculinities that are threatened by masculinities or femininities which are deemed subordinate but which, through every day practice, betray equality. And whilst Moore (1995) quite rightly points out that violence should not be seen as a breakdown in the social order, that is something gone wrong, I would contend that it is in fact just that in another sense: violence represents a breakdown in the 'orders' of gender and interpersonal relationships. We may interpret interpersonal violence as *exactly* the signal that these orders are being threatened with every day experience, the abilities of individuals and the fable of gender difference. The solution to male violence against women is *not* that women conform to traditional conceptions of femininity in order to avoid being battered. Violence is political: men use violence against women because it constitutes an acceptable part of gender relations and intimacy. Society, at most encourages, and at least tolerates, male violence. Men have access to a discourse which normalizes violence. It is this discourse, largely borrowed from socio-biology and psychology, which associates masculinity with violence at the same time that it renders violent women harmless. It is to this latter strategy that the following chapter now turns.

## Notes

1   Whilst such definitions are used by counseling programs for men who batter such as Emerge, public consensus is unlikely to be reached on the efficacy of such an extensive definition.

2   Mills (1985) developed a schema including 'entering a violent relationship', 'managing the violence', 'experiencing a loss of self', 're-evaluating the relationship' and finally 'restructuring the self'. In these stages, women develop and use a variety of coping mechanisms in order to survive the sustained battering.

3   Educational sociology has focused on the interaction of masculinity with social class in such classic text as Paul Willis's (1977) *Learning to Labor* and Pierre Bourdieu's (1977) notion of cultural capital in *Outline of a Theory of Practice*. Other scholars have investigated homosexuality, in such works as Jeffrey Weeks (1996) *Invented Moralities*.

4   In the 1950s only fifteen percent of American homes had televisions whereas today, about ninety-three percent of American homes have one or more televisions. American television programs are the most violent of any Western nation and

consistent evidence suggests that television violence is becoming both more frequent and severe.

5 Children, on average, watch more television than adults. Children watch television before going to school in the morning, at lunch time, after school and in the evening. After school programming especially targets school-aged children. It is more and more common for children to have televisions in their own rooms, decreasing the parental supervision of programs watched. The Nielsen ratings estimate that children aged two to five watch almost twenty-eight hours; children aged six to eleven watch almost twenty-four hours; and children aged twelve to seventeen watch about twenty-one hours of television per week. The average American child spends more time watching television than attending school. Interestingly, there seems to be *more* violence in television programs targeted at children than the majority of programs that are targeted at adults. There are approximately five violent acts per hour in prime time (adult) television, compared with twenty-five violent acts per hour of children's programming.

6 It would be a mistake to think that all feminists are on the anti-pornography 'side'. In fact, many feminists reject any moves towards censorship. Among more prominent feminists on this side of the fence are Betty Friedan, Barbara Ehrenreich, Erica Jong, Kate Millett and Adrienne Rich (Strossen, 1995).

7 Stossen (1995) points out that freedom of expression protects both pornographers who depict women in traditional and demeaning roles but also feminist concerns including abortion, contraception, sexism, lesbianism, homosexuality and same-sex marriage. More recently, anti-censorship feminists highlight the case of *Bad Attitude* in Canada as verification that censorship is counter-productive to women's equality.

8 Activists seeking to censure pornography define pornography quite differently. See MacKinnon (1987).

9 Courts have historically placed great importance on the sexual history of the rape victim and physical evidence that she fought her assailant. This suggests that sexual violence is rarely defined as a 'violent' crime and may only be defined as such when the victim is also 'physically' violated in the form of mutilation or death.

10 The association between heterosexual sex and male aggression towards women is revealed in our very language. Eisler (1996: 222-223) examines the language used by hegemonic and hyper-masculine Western armies which relies heavily on an invocation of heterosexual sex and violence. For instance, Eisler finds that soldiers refer to the penis as a 'gun', the control lever of an aircraft as a 'joy-stick', new weaponry as 'penetrative aids' and nuclear weapons as delivering 'more bang for your buck'. It is not only in the language of war that Eisler finds the association of masculinity with violence against women. Every day words like 'bitch', 'bastard', 'fuck-you' and 'mother-fucker' vividly associate sexuality and violence. Although too extensive to detail here, the now infamous lyrics to various contemporary music groups are 'resplendent' in their association of sexuality and violence. Similarly, Kate Millett's (1969) *Sexual Politics*, explores this specific relation through the examination of classic male novelists such as Henry Miller, Norman Mailer and D.H. Lawrence. Millet calls attention to the passion that these authors direct to maintaining the absolute authority of their male protagonists over the women they encounter, specifically through sexual subordination. No equal relations between the sexes here: only a persistent sexual conquest of women through male violence, ensuring male hegemony.

11    In the United States, for instance, a particular legal case was picked up by the media
      and rocketed marital rape as a societal issue into the public limelight. In 1978 Greta
      Rideout accused her husband, John, of marital rape. In the previous year Oregon had
      joined two other states in removing the common law exemption to rape from its
      criminal code. Prior to this amendment, it was legally impossible for a man to rape his
      wife. The Rideout Case became the first 'test' of Oregon's new law criminalizing
      marital rape for cohabiting couples. The Rideout Case gained national attention and
      dozens of newspaper articles fueled public debate about marital rape. The case
      culminated in a CBS movie-of-the-week *Rape and Marriage: The Rideout Case*. Both
      husband and wife appeared on Good Morning America, local and national newspapers
      and the three major American television networks covered the trial. The media
      coverage focused on a number of issues, the primary one being consent. Traditional
      laws had always held that the marriage contract included, in effect, prior consent to
      sexual intercourse. That is, when a woman consented to marriage, she was *ipso facto*
      consenting to sexual relations with her husband. Such logic was based on the
      assumption that a wife 'belonged' to her husband; that he owned her body. Whilst Mr.
      Rideout's defense attorney tried to frame the argument in terms of prior consent, the
      judge rejected this argument, resulting in a shift of focus to the (now very familiar)
      issue of proving that force was used in order to extract sexual relations. The media
      focused on the assumed ease with which false charges could be brought against
      husbands and the questionable 'moral character' of Greta Rideout.

12    Although wealthy women may be viewed as having escaped the consuming task of
      physical survival, it is also possible to argue that wealthy women were more
      constrained in their daily lives than were poorer women. For it was crucially
      important that wealthy families reproduced heirs, ensured their daughters' chastity
      and proved their wealth through the leisure of their women. A life of leisure for
      wealthy women most often meant stupefying boredom interrupted only by mandatory
      social duties. Poor women, on the other hand, had a much greater access to the
      'public' world. Economic survival alone necessitated that poor women enter access
      public spaces and conduct whatever possible business. This was far from a 'free' life
      however.

13    The explicit exchange of sex services of prostitutes for monetary gain from (most
      often) men usually invites public scorn, especially from women. However, several
      radical feminists as well as prostitute organizations contend that this same exchange
      of services takes place within 'romantic' relationships. Just because this commodity
      exchange is not made explicit does not mean that this is not the structure of these
      relationships. Moreover, it is perhaps, 'more the crassness of this barely disguised
      prostitution – the alienation of cash and cash-related goods on the part of men (who
      have tended to pay for dinner instead of cook it) in exchange for sexual services by
      women – which occasioned the objection, rather than the principle itself' (Kappeler,
      1995: 197).

14    We often find in young children's talk a refreshingly honest acknowledgement that
      goods and services are given on the condition of repayment.

# Chapter 6

# Investing in Difference: Violent Women as Masculinity in Disguise?

Twenty years ago feminist scholars lamented the lack of attention paid to female criminality. However, serious attempts have since been made to both understand the extent of female crime and theorize its etiology. This body of literature reflects an interesting engagement with notions of female criminality and violence. Early studies focused on why there was comparatively so little female crime. The 'deviant female criminal' at that time was most often embodied in the adolescent female delinquent and/or prostitute. In the 1970s this literature was broadened to discussions of battered women who kill their husbands and women who abuse their children or commit filicide. The women's movement and supposed gains in women's equality was predicted to increase women's involvement in crime, particularly white-collar and violent crime. A substantial proportion of more recent feminist research literature has attempted to address this concern as well as document the treatment of female criminals by the legal and psychiatric community. Feminist criminology has also been concerned to highlight biases in criminological theory, which have tended to rest on biological determinist notions of gender as well as a positivist approach to criminality in general. At the same time that men's crime has been explained through the invocation of macro-level explanations such as socio-economic, political and social factors, women's crime, by contrast, has tended to invoke micro-level explanations such as maternal deprivation or mental breakdown (Smart, 1976). These micro-level explananda reveal a common reduction to biological determinism and the 'nature' of women. That is, criminological theory has tended to be eclipsed by gender, creating separate theories of male and female crime.

In this chapter I critically examine the literature on violent women, specifically those women who commit acts of interpersonal violence. As the previous chapters document, the majority of personal violence is committed by males towards known females. Given this fact, the devotion of an entire chapter to the explication of female violence might appear somewhat surprising. One reason to discuss female interpersonal violence in its own right is that whilst non-personal forms of violence are invariably discussed in terms of male participation, female perpetration is most often invoked in discussions of interpersonal violence. But more importantly, I want to argue that it is within discussions of female interpersonal violence that discourses of *gender difference* are most visible. Female interpersonal violence unsettles notions of female passivity and I will be arguing in this chapter that female interpersonal violence particularly invokes a discursive process which attempts to re-establish *gender difference*.

This chapter begins by reviewing statistics concerned with the extent of female violence. A roughly chronological review of the study of female criminality is then provided, with particular attention to the biological assumptions about the 'nature' of femininity. This review concludes with contemporary theories of female criminality, and especially feminist contributions to this discipline. Drawing on research in the areas of women who kill their husbands and women who abuse of kill their children, I provide a critique of some feminist perspectives for what I suggest are bifurcated notions of gender and an unsustainable association between masculinity and violence. The chapter concludes with the implications that these criticisms have for the study of female criminality in general, and female interpersonal violence specifically. Recent gestures towards critical criminology suggest the possibility for alternate conceptualizations of female interpersonal violence which are not limited by *a priori* associations between masculinity and violence.

## The Extent of Female Violence

Perhaps the most common justification for the lack of scholastic attention to female criminality is that it accounts for very little of the violence committed in society. Compared with males, females as a group commit very few violent crimes. In the United States, of the total of 17,657 individuals arrested for murder in 1994, 15,899 (approximately ninety percent) were committed by males compared with 1,758 (approximately ten percent) committed by females (US Bureau of Census, 1996). In 1994 a total of fifty-four Canadian females were accused of attempting or conspiring to murder, compared with 359 males. A total of eighty-three females were accused of sexual assault and 7,911 were accused of non-sexual assault, compared with 4,120 males accused of sexual assault and 44,688 males accused on non-sexual assault (Statistics Canada, 1995). In

1994, in England and Wales, 5,900 women were cautioned for violence against the person offences, compared with 17,600 men. Only 100 women were cautioned for sexual offences compared with 2,900 men (HMSO, 1995). Statistics for 1993 show that there were only 714 female prisoners compared with 13,794 male prisoners in Australia. Only about five percent of Australian prisoners in 1993 were female. In New Zealand, there were a total of 199,517 offenses against the person in 1995; 155,915 (seventy-eight percent) committed by males and 43,602 (twenty-two percent) committed by females (Statistics New Zealand, 1996).

What might be gleaned beyond these broad statistics needs to be understood within the context of statistics on crime more generally. This examination begins with the acknowledgment that the assumed insignificance of female criminality by criminologists and sociologists alike parallels the invisibility of women in other areas of sociology generally (Oakley, 1974). The relatively small number of violent crimes committed by women, low recidivism rates and assumptions about women's greater passivity and conformity combine to produce a cohort considered of little threat to public safety (Shaw, 1995). However, a closer consideration of crime statistics reveals that the proportion of female crime depends on the types of crime discussed.

In an insightful critique of criminological analyses of women and crime, Carol Smart (1976) differentiates between 'sex-specific' and 'sex-related offences'. Sex-specific offenses refer to those statistics which exclude one sex through the legal definition of the offence itself. Infanticide and prostitution are two such cases.[1] Although both men and women can be charged with both offences, the wording of legal definitions of both cases means that very few men are ever charged with either offence. Because both offences are strongly associated with women, we are left with the impression that all prostitutes and parents who kill their children are female. Male prostitution is more commonly conflated with offences concerned with homosexuality. Smart also refers to 'sex-related' offences as those which appear to be predominantly committed by one sex. Shoplifting is a good example. Whilst the literature abounds with statements assuming that shoplifting is a 'women's crime', this is misleading. In actual fact more men than women are apprehended for shoplifting but because comparatively more women shoplift than commit other crimes, this crime is highlighted as a 'women's crime'.

Smart (1976) also points out that non-criminal offences are often considered 'role-expressive' of femininity. In other words, criminologists often study female adolescent delinquents with the assumption that sexuality plays a key role (Smart, 1995). A large set of sex-related offences refer to female sexuality. For instance, female adolescent offences consist largely of running away from home, being considered either beyond the control of parents, or in 'moral danger'. 'Male' offences are more often associated with aggression, as in cases of disorderly conduct, vandalism and loitering. Whilst male delinquency is commonly seen as acting out 'normal' male precociousness, female delinquency is treated with more concern. That female adolescents are scrutinized for sexual 'misconduct' corresponds to the ways in which prostitution is assumed to be a female crime. Assumptions made about female sexuality and its association with immorality is evident in the continued focus on the apprehension of female prostitutes rather than their male clients.

A commonly held belief is that changes in women's position in society, in direct response to the women's movement, has led to a dramatic increase in women's crime.[2] When the FBI reported in 1975 that the number of women arrested in the United States rose by almost 200 per cent between 1960 and 1975, a number of criminologists began to take serious notice of female crime. I wish to return to the association between women's gains in equality and the increase in female crime in a later section, but for now I propose to challenge this claim by looking at studies which have more closely examined the legal system's response to female criminology. Critics of the association point out that women are far more likely to be victims of crime than perpetrators. Moreover, a careful analysis of the criminal justice system reveals that, far from being treated more leniently than men, women are often met with harsher penalties (Chesney-Lind, 1986). The 'double-standard of morality' operating in the criminal justice system does not necessarily work in women's favor (Smart, 1976). Women are more likely to be subject to psychiatric treatment, for instance. Both Terry (1970) and Chesney-Lind (1973) found that female adolescents' behavior was more likely to be defined as sexual offences, adolescent girls were more likely to be subjected to psychiatric treatment and girls were more likely to be institutionalized. Limiting women's identity to that of 'whores' or 'Madonnas' can only consequence a harsher treatment for those girls and women judged to be in the latter category.

Other critics of the view that women's criminality approximates that of men's have conducted closer examinations of arrest and conviction records, concluding that these statistics rely on very small and unreliable numbers which had not been adjusted for changes in the population. A careful analysis of criminal statistics by Steffensmeier (1980) revealed that purported increases in female crime has neglected to acknowledge that male crime has also increased. Moreover, increases in rates of crimes such as shoplifting can be explained by changes in arrest patterns as shop proprietors were more likely to apprehend and charge shoplifters. To the claim that the extent of women's crime tends to be 'masked' because women disproportionately commit crimes within the private sphere of the home is undoubtedly true.

## Violent Women

> ...when women commit violent crimes they are seen to have breached two laws: the law of the land, which forbids violence, and the much more fundamental 'natural' law, which says women are passive carers, not active aggressors, and by nature morally better than the male of the species (Lloyd, 1995, p.36).

Within the rubric of this book, female interpersonal violence in the form of husband killing and child abuse are particularly interesting for two reasons. First, these two forms are very much the focus of both public condemnation. Lloyd (1995) contends the public outrage towards female violence is not accidental: women who harm members of their family act in direct contradiction to fundamental constructions of femininity. Ideas about the family only make sense when mothers and wives are viewed as protective, caring and giving. Second, it is within some feminist literature on these two forms of interpersonal violence that I argue we find a particular discursive maneuvering to transform female heterosexual interpersonal violence into something understandable and non-threatening. Filicide is not strictly part of the rubric of this book because it concerns violence between biologically related individuals and from different age cohorts. However, I have chosen to include it here because filicide shares with partner killing the largest percentage of homicide by women as well as similar public attention.

### *Women who Kill their Male Partners*

Of the few murders that women commit each year the majority are of (ex)partners. In most cases, women who murder their (ex)partners were battered by these men. For instance, in England approximately one hundred men and twenty-five women are convicted each year of killing their partner. About seventy percent of these women who killed their partners were physically abused by them. A similar study of sixteen women who killed their partners found that fourteen had sustained repeated abuse

(Ewing, 1987). It is important to state that a greater number of battered women are killed by their batterers and only a minority of battered women actually kill their abusive partners (Lloyd, 1995).

A series of prominent court cases involving women who had killed their husbands (see Stubbs and Tolmie, 1994) led to increased concern by feminist activists and legal theorists. Research on women who kill their male partners consistently reveals that the majority of these women were victims of their partners' long-term physical, sexual and emotional abuse. For instance, in his early study of one hundred battered women, Gayford (1975) found these women had been beaten with belts and buckles, burned, attacked with knives, razors and broken bottles. All of the women had been bruised, many had suffered fractures and some had limbs dislocated. Similarly, Hilberman and Munson (1977: 460) noted that the sixty battered women in their study had been battered with 'hands, fists, feet, rocks, bottles, phones, iron bars, knives and guns'. Eighty-four percent of the women in Rounsaville and Weissman's (1977) study had been beaten severely enough to require medical treatment. Half of the 420 women studied by Kuhl (1982) reported being beaten at least once a week. Almost half of the women studied by Hoeffler (1982) had been beaten by their husbands whilst pregnant.[3]

Women who kill their male partners and use the self-defense argument basically claim that they had no choice. There is a great deal of corroboration to this claim since most battered women try to get help, usually with little success as many women are not believed by family and friends or the violence is minimized in order to preserve the 'family'. Furthermore, many women do not leave because they lack sufficient money to survive on their own.[4] Battered Woman Syndrome (BWS) emerged in the 1970s in the United States through the work of psychologist Lenore Walker (1979, 1984). Research on BWS and its use to advocate on battered women's behalf has been carried out as a largely radical feminist project. Although most battered women who kill their husbands are convicted or either murder or manslaughter, BWS has been used as a defense in a minority of cases in the United States, Britain, Canada, Australia and New Zealand. There is some evidence to suggest that whilst use of the BWS in court has not been accepted as a defense for murder, it may have some effect on sentencing. For instance, the Minister of Justice in New Zealand recently undertook to review the possibility of lighter sentences, including non-custodial (prison) terms for women who murder violent husbands (New Zealand Herald, 1997). Not surprisingly, the media often highlights the small minority of cases in which women have 'got away with' killing their abusive husbands, leading to the charge that the BWS defense is a wife's 'license to kill' (Jones, 1991).

The problem with the use of the BWS as a defense strategy is that it invokes an *a priori* association between masculinity and violence. This strategy involves focusing on the psychology of the offender (Stubbs and Tolmie, 1994). Given conceptions of the inherent passivity of females, it follows that individual (micro) level explanations are most often invoked. Women are more likely to be labeled psychologically dysfunctional as a result of sustained battering and this dysfunction results in a 'perceived' lack of alternative to killing. The BWS defense tends to downplay the context of battering in which killing is understood by the woman to be the solution on *reasonable* grounds. Women who use the BWS defense run the risk of appearing psychologically disturbed rather than acting reasonably in the context of sustained abuse. This conceptualization has important implications for sentencing as many more women than men are referred to psychiatric treatment.

More importantly, the BWS tends to describe battered women as helpless victims, incapable of violence under 'normal circumstances. Notwithstanding the fact that this image does not fit well with a woman who axes or knifes her husband to death, it serves as a powerful mechanism through which the psychiatric and legal systems maintain a discourse of female passivity and incapacity.[5] In her extensive study of the depiction of female offenders of violent crime in court reports by psychiatrists and probation officers, Hilary Allen (1987) shows that this depiction is gender specific. On average, a greater percentage of court reports on female offenders concern the detailing of her psychology than court reports on male offenders. Court reports of women charged with violent crimes follow a characteristic pattern, according to Allen. In the first place, the female offender is subjected to a greater degree of psychologization in which criminal intention is first denied, her dangerousness is minimized until she is finally returned to the 'sanitized fantasy' of the domestic realm of the home.

Allen compares the psychiatric reports of a male and female defendants charged with murder and arson. The report concerns a man charged with clubbing and hacking to death a casual friend, stealing his electric kettle and shopping bag and then setting fire to his body. The report appears as follows:

> The defendant is of average intelligence. I could elicit no evidence of mental disorder and he is fit to plead. He had consumed a good deal of alcohol on the day of the alleged offence, but he was an habitual drinker and there is no evidence of psychosis (Allen, 1987, p.83).

Compare this statement to one made of a female defendant. This woman attacked and killed the wife of her lover and then set their house on fire killing their two children:

> Olive remembers the early parts of the fight except that she does not remember having her hair pulled out. Her mind is then quite blank until she realized the Jenny had stopped fighting and was seriously wounded. This fact can easily be explained by Olive becoming totally involved in the battle and oblivious to everything around her. She was brought back to her senses, she states, by the sound of one of the children crying. She noticed that a fire had been started in the room, but does not remember starting it. In a daze she fed the child and left the home... Her lack of memory for the events can be explained by her natural defenses in protecting herself. I do not think it at all likely that she planned to commit the crime. The crime, in all probability, developed from the original fight, and the tragic events which followed were caused by the defendant's dissociation from her own feelings, so that she was in an emotionless trance and unable to appreciate what she had done or take steps to prevent a further tragedy from occurring. At this point she could not make responsible decisions. This too was her natural defense against extreme stress. It is a well-known and typical hysterical reaction. (Allen, 1987, p.84-85).

The outcome of this discursive maneuver is ultimately detrimental to women. The assumption that women are incapable of premeditated violent action may result in minimal prison sentences compared with men. However, this 'gain' is traded for a profound denial of women's agency, the repercussions of which varies from a higher likelihood of institutional care, a greater likelihood of being labeled psychologically disturbed or insane and to a greater likelihood of women being returned to their homes in order that they resume the care of their male partners and children. This return to the domestic home 'neither relieves women from the normal constraints of sexual oppression, nor removes the threat of explicitly coercive sanctions in the event of further dissidence' (Allen, 1987: 91). The point is that whilst recognition of the circumstances of much of women's violence against male partners is essential, social justice cannot be served by the categorization of women as only victims. The denial of women's agency, their intentionality, consciousness and culpability necessarily makes women less than fully human subjects. Moreover, there is danger in assuming that all women who kill their partners were battered. It may be that women who are not battered receive particularly harsh treatment by the law because their behavior cannot in any way be mitigated by the acknowledgment of years of abuse.

*Child Abuse and Filicide*

A survey of the 1994 British Home Office statistics reveals, at first glance, a startling figure: the majority of homicide victems were children under the age of one year. Between 1982 and 1989 almost half of the 493 homicides of children committed were by mothers. This constitutes the only form of homicide in which male and female figures are similar.

Discourses of childhood operate coterminously with discourses concerned with motherhood. The 'cult of domesticity' emerged as a configuration of practices, as did ideas about 'bad' mothers and their antithesis, 'good mothers'.[6] The form that the psychiatric evaluation of women who abuse or kill their children takes is complex. 'Bad' mothers are, of course, linked to 'bad' women, as 'good' mothers are only produced by 'good' women. The good mother, like the good woman, is:

> selfless, cheerful, and deodorized. [Her profile does not] include resentment, anger, violence, alienation, disappointment, grief, fear, exhaustion - or erotic pleasure. [She] is ahistorical and apolitical (Ostriker, 1986:179).

Women who kill their children are more likely to face psychiatric treatment than imprisonment, compared with their male counterparts. Moreover, the way in which the courts interpret a woman's intentions has a major impact on the form and length of sentence. Women who are considered 'good' mothers receive lighter sentences than 'bad' mothers. Morris and Wilczynski (1993) argue that women who are cast as 'good mothers' receive lighter sentences primarily because courts are relatively unfamiliar with women accused of homicide. Courts tend to consider mitigating circumstances such as 'current and personal problems' rather than emphasizing the nature of the offence as are done with male offenders. The public, psychiatric and legal opinion concerning what constitutes 'bad' mothering, is linked, unsurprisingly to race, social class, age and employment status. Several researchers have traced the ways in which non-white, working-class women continue to be seen less favorably than their white, middle-class counterparts. Women who work outside the home are particularly vulnerable to charges of neglect and selfishness (Williams, 1991).[7]

**Theorizing Femininity**

Public, legal, criminological and feminist responses to women who kill their male partners or abuse their children reveal a constant preference for the invocation of *gender differences*. That is, to explain female violence, each of these different approaches has tended to focus on the specificity of being female. Therefore, I want to critically examine how femininity is defined and what impact might this definition have on explanations for personal violence.

One strategy to emerge from this paradigm sought to challenge the 'denial and devaluation of specifically feminine virtues and activities by an overly instrumentalized and authoritarian masculinist culture' (Young 1990: 237). Feminist theory argues that the valorization of male activities and masculinity has led to a distortion and devaluation of female activities and femininity within society. The feminist strategy (often called cultural feminism or sexual difference theory), therefore, is to celebrate and demand the recognition of female attributes and activities historically linked with women, especially those surrounding reproduction and mothering. A (re)focus on 'femaleness', the positive values of the female body and traditionally feminine activities, provides the grounding for the recognition of the value of women's work (Alcoff, 1988).

Proponents of the cultural feminist approach tend to focus in on 'woman' specific experiences, practices and thought. These gender-specific ways of knowing, doing and thinking are linked to the body and are the *modus operatus* of women's emancipation. For instance, Rich (1986) argues for a re-affirmation of the female body in order to emancipate women. According to Rich, women's reproductive capacity is exploited and transformed in patriarchal culture through the 'institution of motherhood'. Specific conceptions of the female body are created, expectations are placed on women's behavior, and the identity of women as mothers is constrained. It is as a consequence of this exploitation and constraint that some women abuse or kill their children. In consequence, the potential to bring forth new life is both women's source of power and powerlessness:

> ...[M]aternal power has been domesticated. In transfiguring and enslaving woman, the womb - the ultimate source of this power- has historically been turned against us and itself made into a source of powerlessness (Rich, 1986, p.68).

In essence, women's subordination rests on her bodily potential to reproduce: her specifically female biology. However, the inferior status given to the female body by patriarchal society need not be rejected. Rather women's emancipation rests on '[t]he repossession by women of our bodies [which] will bring more essential change to human society than the seizing of the means of production' (Rich 1986: 285). It is a distinct female essence which is women's ultimate source of power:

> I have become to believe...that female biology - the diffuse, intense sensuality radiating out from clitoris, breasts, uterus, vagina; the lunar cycles of menstruation; the gestation and fruition of life which can take place in the female body - has far more radical implications than we have yet to come to appreciate. Patriarchal thought has limited female biology to its own narrow specifications. The feminist vision has recoiled from female biology for these reasons; it will, I believe, come to view our physicality as a resource, rather than a destiny....We must touch the unity and resonance of our physicality, our bond with the natural order, the corporeal ground of our intelligence (Rich, 1986, p.39-40).

Rich's argument presumes the existence of a number of things. First, there is an assumption that within the female body there exists a pre-given natural essence. Second, this female essence is universal. Various cultural-historical meanings given to the female body are inconsequential relative to this essence. Third, Rich assumes that bodily difference creates specific universal psychologies for men and women and finally; that women's emancipation is universally grounded in physical bodies.

This notion of female consciousness is further developed in the work of Chodorow (1978, 1989) who suggested that men and women develop separate and contrasting gender identities as a result of a particular configuration of mothering. As Chapter Five discussed, Chodorow believed that an infant's early relationship with her/his caretaker (assumed to be the mother or another female) is fundamental to gendered development. It is through this first and primary relationship that the infant begins to develop a sense of self of which gender is a part. The infant may only develop an autonomous sense of self through her/his differentiation from her primary relational object: the mother (Chodorow, 1978). Girls experience a prolonged period of identification and relational sense with the mother because they share the same gender identity based on anatomical difference (that the *lack of* a penis). Boys, on the other hand must separate from their mother in order to develop a separate and different identity: one that is masculine and also includes bodily similarity with their father. For Chodorow, girls establish a sense of self that is relational and continuous due to the experience of this primary relationship which in turn socializes girls to become 'more open and preoccupied with those relational issues that go into mothering' (Chodorow, 1978: 48). Mothering and the desire to mother is therefore, cyclically reproduced. Girls learn to become mothers through a bodily connectedness with their own mothers. This bodily connection in turn facilitates the transference of 'woman' specific qualities developed as a result of the act of mothering.

Chodorow's thesis has informed the arguments of other cultural feminists, especially those of Gilligan (1982) and Harstock (1983). Drawing on the analysis of gender identity development, Gilligan and Harstock suggest that men and women construct specific and contrasting feminine and masculine 'ways of knowing' and thinking. Gilligan's work focuses on moral rationality and argues that men develop a moral rationality based on rights and justice which contrasts with women's feminine ethic of responsibility and care. Gender socialization, conceptualized within the paradigm described above, 'creates in women a relational communal orientation toward others, while it creates in men a more oppositional and competitive mode of relating to others' (Young, 1990: 240). Gilligan argues that male moral reasoning has been valued at the expense of a feminine ethic of care, accounting for a world which is both competitive and uncaring. Women's liberation is thus dependent upon the incorporation and valorization of their ethic of care which will temper dominant masculine values of rationality.

Harstock (1983) argues that in addition to the development of contrasting gender personalities, the sexual division of labor creates different experiences for men and women which in turn produce distinct ways of thinking. Harstock argues that men's labor alienates them from their bodies and the care for others thus determining a way of thinking which is distinctly masculine, defined as 'abstract masculinity, which organizes experience and social relations into binary oppositions in which one term carries greater value than the other' (Young, 1990: 241). Women, on the other hand, are connected to their bodily experiences and their reproductive labor roots them closely to nature. This creates a mode of thought which is relational and values connectedness to others.

This essentialism finds voice in the contemporary works of scholars such as Ruddick and Irigaray. Ruddick (1989, 1994) argues that the act of mothering generates particular modes of thinking or 'maternal thinking' (1989: 24). Maternal thinking produces values which can be beneficial to a politics of peace. Although, Ruddick does not necessarily attribute this kind of thinking to women *per se*, the underlying association is created as this mode of thought is formulated within nurturing activities like mothering; an activity largely performed by women. The work of French feminist Luce Irigaray also centers on 'woman' specific experiences that originate in the female body, particularly female sexuality. Irigaray believes that subjectivity is phallocentric, that is, based on the male, to which all others are compared and defined either positively or negatively (Irigaray, 1985a: 69; Irigaray, 1985b: 133; Grosz, 1989: 104-107). The binary opposition produced by male subjectivity and its comparison with all others consequences a female subjectivity defined only as what is not male: female subjectivity can only be *that which is not* male subjectivity. This conceptualization is mis-conceived (irony intended): men and women are not two halves of one whole but two distinct and separate sexes (Grosz, 1989). This alternative paradigm, for Irigaray, opens a space for the woman to explore and articulate a uniquely female language and subjectivity.

Cultural feminists significantly ground female subjectivity in *a* female body. This universal female body contains *a* universal female essence. Moreover, this essence is articulated as feminine values through an *eternal* maternity which is supposed to incorporate both history and diversity. At the same time, however, women's socially constructed gender identity seems to collapse into a biological female essence which is contained within the female body yet constructed as values through the social act of mothering. In short, sex and gender are entangled:

> We have continued to think of gender in terms of sex: to see it as a social dichotomy determined by a natural dichotomy. We now see gender as the *content* and sex as the *container*. The content may vary...but the container is assumed to be invariable because it is part of nature and 'nature does not change'. Moreover, part of the nature of sex is seen to be its *tendency to have a social content*/to vary culturally (Delphy, 1993, p.3).

The cultural feminist assertion that there exists distinct feminine virtues and a female nature does little to challenge dominant conceptions of 'woman'. Rather it attempts to valorize 'woman' by the very act of women providing these definitions. As a consequence, 'woman' is described as a universal, definable identity distinguishable from 'man', concomitantly, 'woman' means 'mother', through the grounding of women's emancipation on a female particularity rooted in procreation.

Cultural feminism is noticeably silent with regard to women who abuse children. It is clear that the essential notions of women as caring are not easily reconciled with child abuse and without direct theorizing by cultural feminists on this issue, it is difficult to conceptualize a coherent theory from this perspective. Indeed, Chodorow (1989) describes a 'moral paralysis' with which maternal violence is dealt. Whereas male violence has been both described and opposed, female violence remains enigmatically silenced.

The other general approach to feminist theory on mothering is represented in the works of radical feminists. In *From Here to Maternity,* Ann Oakley (1986) proposes that a 'myth of motherhood' pervades society. In this myth, mothers are completely satisfied with the tasks of parenthood. Children are an unwavering joy and women gain ultimate contentment through mothering. The reality of motherhood is an extremely tiring and largely thankless occupation, unpaid and largely un-credited. It is no coincidence that most children are killed within the first year of life, a time of tremendous strain on parents.[8] For radical feminists such as Catherine MacKinnon (1987), the 'selfless caring' purported to exemplify the mother is no more than a learned behavior of women who are victims of a patriarchal society that chains women to unpaid domestic labor. The idea that a woman's violence towards her children may be the result of the mother's own oppression experienced within a patriarchal societal and family structure is found in the work of Rich (1986) who describes several cases of mothers who violently abused and murdered their children. She contextualizes this violence within patriarchal society: these women become mothers through rape, ignorance, poverty, no access to safe, affordable and reliable birth control and/or failed abortion. 'Patriarchal violence' thus occurs through the mother.

Radical feminism has been criticized for what is viewed as a devalorization of women's experiences of motherhood. This criticism must be tempered, in my view, by the recognition that it is in radical feminist theory that one of the only substantial bodies of knowledge about female child abusers is found. My difficulty in accepting radical feminist approaches to women who abuse or kill their children has less to do with their supposed devaluation of motherhood and more to do with a continued lack of agency attributed to women. This is exemplified by the large focus of radical feminist theory on why battered women 'fail' to protect their children. It is quite valid to point out that women are held responsible for the functioning of the family and the protection of children. Roberts, for instance, relates how children are effectively held hostage within the institution of the family and mothers' commitment to their children effectively maintains women's subordination: 'if children are the chains that keep women from freedom, it is not surprising that mothers sometimes strike at those chains' (1995: 113). Whilst similarities have been drawn between the abuse of women by their male partners and the abuse of children by their mothers, Roberts resists this analogy by stating that 'the power involved in these forms of abuse are different: maternal child abuse may be at once a form of oppression and of opposition to the oppressive mothering role' (1995: 114). In the case of a woman who abuses or kills a male partner who has savagely abused her over the course of their relationship, it may be reasonable to say that her behavior is mitigated by her oppression. However, I find it more problematic to make this assertion about women who abuse or kill their children. That women as a group are oppressed within the institution of the family is a largely uncontested matter: to theorize that women abuse children solely (or mainly) as the result of patriarchal oppression is another matter. Certainly it is true that women 'violate gender norms' when they abuse or abandon their children, but it is surely important to recognize that women's 'resistance' in this case seems to be predicated on the abandonment, abuse or death of children. I think that Roberts's own caution to radical feminists who identify with women who abuse their children warrants emphasis. Whilst she advocates such an identification to understand the oppressive system in which women live, this identification must not deny women's agency and responsibility in their choice of forms of resistance which harm other people. And again, whilst evidence suggests that the majority of women who abuse their children live within abusive relationships with their partners, this theory fails to adequately explain those women who abuse their children outside such oppression.

### Theorizing Femininity and Heterosexual Interpersonal Violence

Whilst a great deal of work has been done on the study of male criminality, relatively little attention has been paid to female criminality. The early period of the study of female criminality is largely characterized by the works of Lombroso and Ferrero (1895) and Thomas (1907, 1967). These theories subscribe to biological determinism and generalities are made about men's and women's 'nature'.[9] For instance, women's low crime rate (compared with men's) was seen as proof of either female moral superiority (innate virtue) or of women's greater submission and weakness (Leonard, 1982), a supposition that still resonates with popular discourse today. For instance, the invocation of social evolution was used by Pike in 1987 to explain how women's lower crime rate was the result of women's lack of physical strength and consequent learned non-criminal behavior.

Notwithstanding Cesare Lombroso's (1895) devotion of an entire text to the study of female crime, the 'father' of criminology believed that women were, in general, non-criminal because of their innate passivity.

'Normal' women were like children; less intelligent than men and incapable of the cunning required of the criminal. Lombroso and Ferrero's (1895) *The Female Offender* was based on a study of women criminals (mainly prostitutes) which concluded that many more men than women were 'born' criminals, atavistic throwbacks to a less evolved human. The lower percentage of female criminals showing these 'atavistic characteristics' was explained by the theory that men were more evolved than women. Because women were less evolved, they had less far to degenerate (Smart, 1976). The 'normal' woman was characterized by her 'reserve, docility and sexual apathy', whilst the female criminal was masculinized (Lombroso and Ferrero, 1895: 297). The emphasis on sexual passivity is particularly revealing, given the enormous percentage of the female criminal population who were serving sentences for prostitution or moral 'indecency' of some sort. Given that the 'natural' (read good) woman was sexually apathetic and generally reserved, it is of little wonder that any woman actively engaged in any form of sexual behavior was seen as deviant. Heidensohn (1995) observes that female 'deviancy' largely concerns sexuality. This focus on female sexuality was by no means unique to Lombroso and Ferrero, as the later study by Glueck and Glueck (1935) attests. Their study, entitled *Five Hundred Delinquent Women* concluded that the vast majority of the women had committed 'acts of sexual or personal immorality' and that most of these women were 'mentally defective'. The social-economic circumstances of these women were noted in extensive life-histories, but the link between extreme poverty and prostitution to earn a living was never made (Leonard, 1982).

Just as Lombroso's theory rested on the innate masculinity of criminal behavior, so too did Thomas's *Sex and Society* (1907) and *The Unadjusted Girl* (1967). For Thomas, women were defined by their domestic roles as wives and mothers. And like Lombroso, Thomas believed that men were the more highly evolved of the human species, women being closer in development to children (as well as the lower classes and non-white peoples). In his later work on delinquent girls, Thomas argued that behavior was directed through human 'wishes' derived from biological instincts. Given women's 'predisposition' for the nurturance of offspring, women possess a greater need and desire for love than men (Smart, 1976). Therefore, the particular forms that women's criminality takes reflects this greater search for love, comfort and attention. Thus it is not surprising that Thomas focuses on the sexual 'promiscuity' of female adolescent delinquents.

This is the heritage of analyses of female criminality. Contemporary theories of female criminality reveal a persistence of biological explanations which promote discourses of *gender difference*. In *The Criminality of Women* (1950) Pollak was able to combine an emphasis on biological factors found in Lombroso's work with the social factors found in Thomas's work. To corroborate his theory, Pollak makes reference to the common complaint by men that women are deceitful. Pollak not only believes this deceitfulness of women is inherent, but that it derives from the heterosexual sex act in which women are able to fake orgasm in a way not available to men. Pollak takes this 'biological fact' and adds a psychological implication: because women are physically able to fool men, women develop a general attitude towards deceit and women become proficient liars (Pollak, 1950). The reality of women's lower status in marriage, the power differential between men and women and the invisibility of marital rape do not figure in this conception (Smart, 1976).[10] (Early as this theory was, it has definite resonance with contemporary feminist approaches to explaining women's abuse of their children as I will discuss in a later section).[11] The potential importance of Pollak's work, in challenging biological notions and assumptions about women's inherent passivity and insisting that female criminality be taken seriously is lost in the largely non-empirical, biological generalizations of his theory. Interestingly, Pollak's thesis was to find company in later scholastic interest on the effects of the women's movement on rates of female criminality.

Gisela Konopka's *The Adolescent Girl in Conflict* (1966) details the accounts of girls institutionalized for delinquency from case histories, observation and interviews. Konopka details the apparent absence of love and maternal bonding in these girls' upbringing which leads to emotional instability and later sexual delinquency in particular (Smart, 1976). Moreover, Konopka uncritically accepts that these girls are deviant, subscribing to legal and institutional definitions of delinquency and deviancy. This focus on individual-level explanations allows Konopka to differentiate between 'normal' (non-delinquent) girls and 'abnormal' (delinquent) girls, thus structuring the argument that 'normal', well-adjusted girls cannot be delinquent.

Cowie, Cowie and Slater's study *Delinquency in Girls* (1968) superficially appears to address the issue of female criminality in its own right. But a closer examination reveals a strong positivist approach echoed in Lombroso and Ferrero's work. In their study of delinquent girls, Cowie, Cowie and Slater differentiate the 'delinquent' girl from the 'normal' girl through a list of variables including lower intelligence, impaired physical health and less attractive physical appearance (as defined by the researchers). So the researchers are able to state that 'delinquent girls more often than boys have other forms of impaired physical health; they are noticed to be oversized, lumpish, uncouth and graceless, with a raised incidence of minor physical defects' (Cowie, Cowie and Slater, 1968: 166-167). Rather than accord social, structural and class factors importance in their contribution to these variables (for example, middle class girls have more money to spend on their appearance and can afford better diets), the researchers preferred to prioritize psychological and physiological etiological factors. Moreover, in comparing female and male delinquency, Cowie, Cowie and Slater argued that boys are more affected by their environments which is one of the leading causes of their delinquency. Girls, on the other hand are more likely to become delinquent from a biological predisposition towards crime, that is evident only in 'abnormal' girls. It is not long before Cowie, Cowie and Slater refer to the chromosomal difference between males and females, suggesting that it is the Y chromosome that is associated with delinquency. In linking criminality with masculinity, it follows that female delinquents are more 'masculine' than their non-delinquent feminine counterparts.

## Challenging the Link Between Feminism and Heterosexual Interpersonal Violence

If, at first, feminist theory seemed reluctant to embrace findings of female interpersonal violence, this reluctance has been more recently eclipsed by work within feminist criminology and critical criminology. That feminist criminology has sustained its focus on male oppression of women is hardly surprising given both the prevalence and seriousness of wife assault and its historical relegation as a matter of domestic rather than criminal concern. However, the often subtle omission of female violence is, as a consequence, found in several such analyses. For instance, Sue Lees (1993: 227) analyses female understanding and experience of sexuality and relationships with boys, asserting that 'male violence is condoned whilst female anger is outlawed'. She goes on to say that girls are sometimes bullies as well and 'sometimes fight each other' but these forms of female violence are not accorded any sustained discussion.

Part of the insistence by feminists that wife assault be considered criminal stems from a need to recognize the volition involved in abuse as opposed to the deferral of responsibility to such factors as violence in the family of origin and consumption of alcohol. In short, feminist criminology has highlighted the salience of power relations (at both structural and individual levels) in acts of personal violence. As Liz Kelly (1992: 51) points out 'recognizing the deliberateness of abusers' behavior is disturbing. It is more comfortable to believe abusers or their partners are merely repeating what they learned in childhood'.

Research on lesbian battering (for instance, Renzetti, 1992; Taylor and Chandler, 1995; Lobel, 1986) has directly confronted the subject of female interpersonal violence, necessitating the acknowledgment that partner abuse is not confined to heterosexual relationships and the supposed inherent patriarchal oppression to be found therein. The stereotypes of sado-masochism and butch-femme performance used to explain lesbian battering through this patriarchy-oppression framework are particularly critiqued. Taylor and Chandler (1995) point out that butch-femme lesbians do not simply 'ape' male-female roles and it is often the publicly femme lesbian who is the perpetrator of abuse.

This research on lesbian battering as well as increased concern with the conceptualization of women as victims necessitates a re-thinking of assumptions concerning the role of gender in interpersonal violence. On the one hand, a substantial amount of research clearly suggests that men are far more violent in intimate relationships than women. So a theory of interpersonal violence needs to account for what appears to be the clear association between gender and violence. On the other hand, without falling into the conceptual trap of understanding women as helpless victims without agency, this theory must embrace recent findings of female interpersonal violence. Kappeler (1995) asserts that feminist analyses of power and the discourse applied to women's oppression and men's dominance is applied both wholly and individually. That is, individual men and women, and their behaviors towards each other, are defined *by their gender*. So women are, by definition, victims and men are perpetrators. We tend not to look beyond this equation because gender identity identifies and defines the individuals' relationship. Kappeler (1995: 115) argues that through a process of 'discursive reconstruction' we accommodate instances of female desire for power, control and their behaviors of manipulation into a paradigm of female victimization and selflessness. New theories of gender work towards re-conceptualizing violence as neither inherently male or female.

The search for an explanation of non-defensive female violence is developed in Anne Campbell's work on female adolescent gangs (1984) and later work on adult experiences of interpersonal and stranger violence (1993). Through her discussions with female gang members, Campbell is able to dispel the myth that violence is an exclusively male domain. Critical of earlier work on female delinquency which tended to emphasize girls' apparent immorality, dependence on boyfriends and male gangs, and psycho-social problems developed in childhood, Campbell insists that female gang behavior be examined in its own right. I want to focus attention on Campbell's more recent work on women and men's 'social representations' of violence. Campbell interviewed two single-gender groups about their experiences of violence. Male group members described participating in violent incidents in terms of the behaviors, rather than emotions, invoked by the experiences. Physical fighting was described in terms of 'not backing down', that is, that it challenged male conception of masculinity. Most of the men in the group described violent incidents in terms of avoiding being called cowardly. The men's' narratives focused on their social relations as hierarchically structured and violence as a response to any sort of challenge to this hierarchy. Violence, for these males, is about power and control. The purpose of violence and aggression is to gain (or maintain) power over another person.

According to Campbell, women most often described violence in terms of the emotions of anger and frustration. These women described situations in which they felt very angry and *lost control* of themselves and acted violently. Violence was the *expression* of this loss of control, this last straw. Campbell interprets this data to suggest that the social representation of violence is gendered. Campbell agues that men's violence is instrumental in that it achieves power over another person or situation. Women's violence, on the other hand, is expressive; an overt demonstration to another person of feeling very out of control. When women are violent it is a cry for help, not the expression of a desire for power over someone else.

What I find most interesting about these narratives is the different attributions given to females and males for their violent behavior. Campbell analyzes the men as using an 'instrumental social representation' compared with the 'expressive social representation' chosen by the women. What this reveals is not so much whether men and women commit different kinds of violent acts but rather the expectation we have that violence is necessarily gendered. In other words, there is a discursive process involved in our conceptualization of the relationship between violence and gender: we expect women to emphasize caring relationships and men to emphasize hierarchical, instrumental relations; women and men also differentially use language to express this expectation as well as make sense of their experiences of their own violent behavior. Given that the men and women in this study often described similar acts of aggression and violence, and yet had quite different ways of explaining this behavior, this seems to suggest that there is a discursive process in operation. This is interesting, also, because Campbell herself does not seem to see the possibility of this analysis, preferring instead to provide a rather standard analysis predicated on *a priori* conceptualization of gender.

This point is worth laboring. Research discussed earlier in this chapter suggests that female violence is often ignored, trivialized or otherwise rendered harmless. Male violence, in contrast, receives attention, often in the form of tolerance (as in 'boys will be boys') or outright acceptance. Indeed, it is clear that society expects a certain degree of aggression and violence from males as this behavior is an intricate part of the male social script. On the other hand, when women commit acts of personal violence, society is faced with behavior that is in direct contravention to valued gendered social scripts. Women's violence if often interpreted as the product of mental disturbance: the violent woman becomes the *victim* of forces beyond her control. The ways in which the criminal justice system working in conjunction with the psychiatric discipline discursively maneuver the violent woman into a position of passivity has been discussed earlier (see Allen, 1987). The consequences of making women passive non-agents is to further silence female volition. Note that even in cases in which women are convicted of serial murders, these women are often relegated to the role of accomplice to the male (often a boyfriend or husband) who is seen as the real agent of the violent acts. As Smart (1976: 2) remarks, 'we have...no shortage of material on such areas of maternal deprivation or insanity and mental breakdown amongst women'. Thus, society provides a very narrow discourse with which to situate the violent woman.

One of the ways in which many analyses of female criminality proceed is to begin with the premise that certain 'male' characteristics are associated with criminality (toughness, isolation, aggression, 'macho', independence) and therefore certain 'female' characteristics (passivity, conformity, dependence, emphasis on relationships) are associated with non-offending. An *a priori* association is made between masculinity and violence. Analyses then proceed to locate the 'cause' of female criminality in how 'masculine' the female offender is.

It is often assumed that women's primary goals are relational whilst men's primary goals are economic and work-related. This assumption is based on generalizations in which all women (and all men for that matter) are attributed the same needs and goals. However, the argument is still more subtle. We equate femininity with passivity and masculinity with aggression. We also assume that women's relationships are structured around a non-hierarchical ethic of care. This supposed female preferencing of relationships necessarily implies that these relationships are premised around selfless caring. Precisely because of these powerful *a priori* associations, a certain discursive maneuvering often takes place in which girls and women are able to talk freely about what they desire and what they do 'for the sake of the relationship'; rather than about the desire to have control or power over the other person. This discursive maneuvering shifts the focus from the individual behavior of the woman to the nebulous behavior of the relationship:

> I can want to have a relationship, whereas wanting to have a person would be suspiciously close to wanting to own and rule that person. I can make the relationship my need, whereas needing another person might make it clear that this means using that person for my need. Not only does this look unselfish, but in being "willing to take more responsibility than the partner for initiating the relationship and keeping it going" we think moreover that we are taking the sacrificial part, carrying the greater share of the "work" (Kappeler, 1995, p.115-116).

This discursive maneuver creates a problem. Analyses of female interpersonal violence tend to focus on social relations without a similar emphasis on individual desire and agency. This has consequenced a paradox for feminist scholarship on violence. The explanation we often offer for female violence is that it is a response to male violence. It is self-defense, either immediate or projected. As Campbell (1993: 179) notes, 'wife beating has become so intimately bound up with feminist ideology that there is a real reluctance to focus on the other side of the coin - physical aggression by wives'. In this sense, women forever remain only the responders to male agency, even if that response is resistance in the form of violent action: '[w]here the woman's behavior towards others is the issue, we speak of others' behavior towards the woman' (Kappeler, 1995: 78).

The other related response consists of attributing female acts of interpersonal violence to the adoption of masculine social scripts. This is a rather more subtle attribution than the traditional emphasis on biology. An analysis of research in this area finds fewer studies hypothesizing that violent women have higher levels of testosterone or an extra Y chromosome.[12] Instead, research now tends to hypothesize that violent women are more 'masculine' than non-violent women (Naffin, 1985). Now we look for the ways in which girl delinquents exhibit 'boyish behavior' and violent women practice male social scripts. What this research does is test 'for the presence of 'masculinity' or the absence of 'femininity' and attempted to relate these traits to criminal propensity. The idea that female crime is a mode of expressing 'femininity' has not, however, been pursued (Naffin, 1985: 379).

A workable approach to female criminality, then, requires the structural context in which female criminality and interpersonal violence more particularly, takes place must inform all explanations of this form of female criminality. Radical feminist contributions to this understanding continue to be invaluable. The tendency to attach either the 'victim' or 'masculine' label to women must also be resisted. In either case, this assignation reveals the broader conceptualization of gender as a priori associated with violence. Finally, feminist theory needs to explore the possibility of developing an understanding of female criminality outside of the auspices of criminology:

> The problem which faces criminology is not insignificant...and arguably its dilemma is even more fundamental than that facing sociology. The whole raison d'etre of criminology is that it addresses 'crime'. It categorizes a vast range of activities and treats them as if they are all subject to the same laws - whether laws of human behavior, genetic inheritance, of economic rationality or development and so on...The thing that criminology cannot do is deconstruct 'crime'. It cannot locate rape or child sexual abuse in the domain of sexuality, nor theft in the domain of economic activity, nor drug use in the domain of health. To do so would be to abandon criminology to sociology, but more importantly it would involve abandoning the idea of a unified problem which requires a unified response - at least at the theoretical level (Smart, 1995, p.39).

Acts of female interpersonal violence particularly invoke, both publicly and within most sociological and criminological theorizing, a strong sense of 'gender trouble' (Butler, 1990) which consequences a process of discursive maneuvering to render women's violence either silent, a response to male violence, or the practice of male social scripts. Each of these alternatives simultaneously reproduces the same *a priori* link between masculinity and violence, and the fundamental notion that women cannot be agents in their own right.

## Notes

1    Throughout this text the term 'gender' is used to emphasize the point that gender discourses create sex. See Hird (2000b).

2    These works include Otto Pollak's (1961) *The Criminality of Women;* Freda Adler's (1975) *Sisters in Crime;* Rita James Simon's (1975) *Women and Crime*; Richard Demings (1977) *Women: The New Criminals*; Freda Adler and Rita Simon's (1979), *The Criminology of Deviant Women;* and, Freda Adler's, (1981) *The Incidence of Female Criminality in the Contemporary World.*

3    In Lenore Walker's (1984) landmark study of 435 battered women, fifty-nine percent reported being raped by their partners. Many battered women report being forced to engage in 'unusual sex acts' including 'being forced to insert objects in their vaginas, to engage in group sex, have sex with animals and participate in bondage and other sadomasochistic activities' (as the quotes from Kennedy Bergen's 1995 study discussed in Chapter Five attest). Others report that their partners raped them in front of their children. Battered women also report sustaining high levels of psychological abuse from their partners. Interestingly, Walker found the women in her study shared each of the eight forms of abuse that Amnesty International defines as 'psychological torture' including social isolation; exhaustion stemming from deprivation of food and sleep; monopolization of perception manifested in obsessive or possessive behavior; threats (including threats of death) against the woman, her relatives and friends; humiliation, denial of power, and name calling; administration of drugs and alcohol, induction of altered states of consciousness and indulgences given with the intent of making the woman believe that the abuse would cease.

4    Battered women and their children are often forced to flee their home city, necessitating the securing of a new source of income (often substantially lower) and schooling for the children. Many women who do leave their husbands flee to a battered women's shelter. There are far fewer shelters available than required and can only provide temporary respite. Children of battered women are often extremely frightened and suffer from a variety of psychological and physical problems.

5    Research has shown that the BWS has actually worked *against* some women in court by suggesting that women who fight back are not helpless and therefore had other recourses than kill their husbands (Stubbs and Tolmie, 1994).

6    Readers interested in the development of domesticity as an ideology and the development of ideas about 'bad' and 'good' mothers are referred to Ashe and Cahn 'Child abuse: A problem for feminist theory', in Weisberg's, (1996) *Applications of Feminist Legal Theory to Women's Lives: Sex, Violence, Work and Reproduction.*

7    The recent case of Louise Woodward reveals this bias. Whilst a great deal of concern was shown towards this nanny who was charged with murdering the infant in her care, a significant number of reports condemned Deborah Eappen for choosing to work outside the home instead of devoting herself full-time to the care of her child. Interestingly, little attention was paid to the fact that Sunil Eappen also 'chose' to work outside the home, rather than care for his child.

8    Roberts (1995) points out that men abandon their children by leaving them with their mother whereas women's abandonment of their children is much more likely to receive legal attention. In cases where the child is beaten to death, the families into which these babies are typically born feature wife assault, financial problems, chaotic and violent family history and other children.

9    What also identifies these early theories is their reliance on heavily stereotyped and denigratory assumptions about women. Around this time, Freud attributed women's criminality to those minority of women who had not adjusted properly to their roles as wives and mothers (Simon, 1975). According to Freud, 'normal' women reconcile their envy of the male phallus by becoming mothers and wives, whilst female criminals expressed their envy of males in the 'masculinity complex'. Freud contended that women generally had both a lower moral sense and a greater jealous capacity which was reflected in women's three fundamental traits of passivity, masochism and narcissism (Millett, 1969).

10    Pollak goes on to say that the 'masked' crimes that women commit are most often directed at their male partners and children whom women can easily harm due to the privacy of the home. In fact, Pollak describes in some detail how women might poison the food which they prepare for their husbands. It is reasonable to expect that a certain amount of female perpetrated child abuse does go unreported. However, there is no reason to believe that men's abuse of children is always reported either. Pollak also contends that whilst women report their abuse at the hands of men, men are more reluctant to report their abuse by women. Whilst this theory finds support in public perceptions that men are not 'cry babies' and take abuse without 'snitching' in fact research suggests that men are more likely to report abuse by female partners than women are to report abuse by male partners (Steinmetz, 1977). Pollak further argues that men deceive themselves about women's true nature which has a propensity towards deceit and evilness. Whilst Pollak seems to admit that at least some of this evilness may stem from women's unequal treatment in society, he is able to turn this unequal treatment to women's comparative advantage: women attempt to avenge their inferior status on those individuals whom they perceive are the cause of their oppression, such as their husbands and children (Smart, 1976).

11    Pollak is even able to turn menstruation into a means by which to justify his theory of higher levels of female crime: women, it seems, commit crime as an act of vengeance for their inferior status which is revealed monthly to them at the onset of menstruation (Smart, 1976). Pollak's argument depends, of course, on the Freudian notion that women associate menstruation with their lack of phallus and failure to be men and that women self-identify as inferior.

12    Interestingly, modern socio-biological explanations have found rejuvenation in research on pre menstrual syndrome. For a critique of this research see Morris (1987) *Women, Crime and Criminal Justice*, and Lloyd (1995) *Doubly Deviant, Doubly Damned*.

# Chapter 7

# Engendering Violence?

No single theory of violence can adequately explain all forms of violence. This book has amassed empirical research on childhood, adolescence and adult heterosexual interpersonal violence, in order to fashion a particular critique. I have argued that gender is considered to be one of the most significant markers of individuals in society. That is, children learn from a very early age to differentiate between people based on their gender. The 'other' gender is not only considered different, but indeed opposite. Small differences between genders are represented as large, irreconcilable differences such that the world is divided into men on the one hand and women on the other. A discourse of 'us' and 'them' provides a fertile ground on which to facilitate the use of violence. I have further argued that gendered social relations operate through heteronormative discourse. This discourse further alienates women from men as it structures particular social relations based on sexual coercion.

This final chapter seeks to further explore the relationship between gender, identity and interpersonal relationships. These are rich concepts: each has been the subject of texts in their own right. I thus want in this brief summary to tease out some of the major points of these themes as they relate to the current study of heterosexual interpersonal violence.

## Gender

Chapter Two examined the various theoretical shifts concerning our understanding of gender. Although this would seem to call for a serious questioning of biological assumptions about gender, what we find is a particular resilience of biological, and more recently psychological discourses.[1] These discourses are predicated on the notion that gender exists and that definitive 'masculine' and 'feminine' traits are measurable. Chapter Five discussed a number of studies which begin with the assumption that males are typically seen to be more assertive, competitive and aggressive whilst females are considered to be more nurturing, empathic and passive. Chapter Six argued that female criminality is most often explained through a discursive manoeuvre which renders violent women either 'masculine' and dangerous, or 'feminine' and harmless. Indeed, interpersonal violence research generally sustains the notion that violence is a masculine characteristic; women who are violent must somehow either be victims of male violence or more masculine than women in general.

Interpersonal violence is certainly not the only behavior that invokes such discursive reconstruction. We attribute all sorts of characteristics, traits and even whole personalities to women and men as groups. One of the most common attributions is reflected in the work of Campbell (1991), discussed in Chapter Six in which women were 'expressive' whilst men were 'instrumental'. Public discourse also abounds with these associations, as in disparaging comments about 'women drivers' and statements such as 'boys will be boys'. Robert Connell (1987) provides an insightful critique of psychological 'sex difference' research which Naffin has characterized as relying 'more on popular stereotypes than on systematic inquiry for their conceptions of the alleged personality differences between the sexes' (1985: 366). This body of research typically assesses supposed differences between women and men on a whole host of attributes: sensitivity to touch, verbal expression, spatial organization and intelligence to name a few. Connell notes that 'significance testing', focuses on the probability that some difference exists between the two groups (women and men) rather than the size or validity of this difference.

Because it is differences that researchers are looking for (and it is gender *differences* rather than *similarities* which are more likely to be published), there has been a tendency to emphasize differences rather than similarities between women and men. More recently, a number of studies have begun to acknowledge that the sorts of group differences expected in gender difference research are few: most characteristics are shared by men and women and there are many areas in which the differences between men or between women are as great or greater than the differences between women and men (Spellman, 1988; Fausto-Sterling, 1992; Lorber, 1994).

This acknowledgment has led to a movement away from unitary notions which define that 'men are...' and 'women are...' (although we still find these statements in the literature on heterosexual interpersonal violence) and towards non-unitary notions of gender. The most popular revision of gender theories has, nevertheless, proven uninspiring. In this research, men and women are understood as positioned along a continuum of human traits. However, these supposedly human traits are nevertheless defined *a priori* as masculine or feminine. Psychology uses a number of measures of 'masculinity' and 'femininity', such as the Minnesota Multiphasic Personality Inventory (MMPI) and the Bem Sex-Role Inventory. Researchers using such scales define traits as 'feminine' or 'masculine' when a statistically significantly higher number of one gender than the other assign themselves to particular traits. But how traits become included on these scales in the first place often has to do with the traditional beliefs of the researchers themselves. For instance, in their study of aggression, Loy and Norland (1981) defined masculinity as paying for dates, fixing cars and taking on the role of family earner whilst femininity was defined as the expectation of being a homemaker and is interested in children. Part of the problem is the way in which these scales are designed.[2] Because masculinity and femininity are considered to be separate homogenous entities (that is the difference between genders is taken to be greater than the differences within genders), they are placed at opposite ends of any scale. So, for instance, when aggression is measured, those who report the least amount of aggression are defined as feminine (even if they are male) whilst those reporting the most amount of aggression are defined as masculine (even if they are female). Attempts to overcome this problem have tended to create 'androgyny' scales which use separate scales for each gender such that an individual might score highly on both masculine and feminine traits.

But the problem with measuring gender is more serious than the refining of gender-difference scales. The problem is that we remain unable to say just exactly what femininity and masculinity are. Ann Constantinople notes that 'both theoretically and empirically they seem to be among the muddiest concepts in the psychologist's vocabulary'. Elaborating further she notes:

> we are dealing with an abstract concept that seems to summarize some dimension of reality important for many people, but we are hard pressed as scientists to come up with any clear definition of the concept or indeed any unexceptionable criteria for its measurement (Constantinople, 1973, p.390).

Whilst psychology continues to struggle with the quantification of gender, some recent literature from sociology has moved towards a 'performative gender' theory (see Chapter Two). Rather than take as given the structure of gender, this literature begins with a philosophical analysis of how gender has been conceived of in terms of an *a priori* polarity. We find in this literature the revelation of the fundamental way in which humans structure their reality.

It is through this system of bifurcation that the meaning of gender itself is established. We can only know what 'man' is through its *opposition*, 'woman'; the female is everything that is absent from the male and *vice versa*. But despite daunting conceptual limitations, we remain reticent to abandon the concept of gender in toto. Recent terminology applies instead an assemblage of masculinities and femininities.[3] Connell (1987) defines masculinity as a sort of umbrella term which signifies a set of social relations amongst men structured hierarchically and founded on the subordination of women.[4] It consists of a hierarchy achieved through social relations that transcend 'brute' power to the very organization of private life and cultural relations. Hegemonic masculinity is not a fixed character type. Where gender, class, race, ethnicity, age and so on intersect, different masculinities will occupy hegemonic positions. Subordinated masculinities (and femininities) are not only identified by power relations 'but also in relation to a division of labor and patterns of emotional attachment, psychological differentiation and also institutional differentiation as part of collective practices' (Newburn and Stanko, 1994: 3).

Hegemonic masculinity is strongly implicated with heterosexuality (Connell, 1995). Homosexual masculinities must necessarily come at the bottom of masculinity hierarchies. The number of men who actually practice hegemonic masculinity is very small as it is quite difficult for men to live as the 'top' men in any culture. Some of the men who do not practice hegemonic masculinity instead practice what is called 'complicit masculinity'. It involves 'masculinities constructed in ways that realize the patriarchal dividend, without the tensions or risks of being the front-line troops of patriarchy' (Connell, 1987: 79). These men comply with hegemonic masculinity as they benefit from the subordination of females. Other masculinities are more 'marginal' to society in the sense that they protest and conflict with the various hegemonic and complicit masculinities. Gay masculinity would be an obvious example of a masculinity of the margin. Another feature of the theory of multiple masculinities and femininities is that any individual female will not necessarily object to hegemonic masculinity. Indeed, any number of females might find this form of masculinity more 'familiar and manageable'.

Females, like males, can express a range of femininities as the research explored in Chapters Three, Four and Six demonstrates. One choice is that of 'emphasized femininity' (Connell, 1987). This form of femininity includes females who practice femininity in ways that confirm traditional gender boundaries. When girls and women pretend they are stupid in the company of males, they are practicing emphasized femininity.

There are, of course, a wide variety of femininities: mothers, lesbians, career women, child-free women, single women and prostitutes. We tend to personify particular women as representations of various femininities. The more these women appear to practice a non-traditional femininity, the greater the probability that they will be defined as deviant. Hilary Clinton, Madelaine Albright and Margaret Thatcher have often been called 'men in skirts', a term signalling our discomfort with signs that a gender boundary has been crossed.

We may suppose that there are certain 'truths' about masculinity and femininity; 'truths' which are often described by their proponents as timeless, incontrovertible and non-negotiable. Performativity, on the other hand, allows the possibility of change and transformation. This opportunity does not necessarily result in a more tolerant gender performance: the possibility also exists to affirm conventional and restricted gender practices. It is to the relationship between gender as a performative concept and the cultural milieu in which this performance takes place that I now turn.

**Agency and Power**

The emerging literature identifies gender as a fluid, socially subjective concept that exists only in the context of practice. If we are now to understand gender as a set of practices to be performed, we need to explicate the relationship between performance and societal structures. To what extent does society limit individuals' possible gender performances? This is an age-old debate between structure and agency: to what extent do humans act through free will and to what extent are our actions circumscribed by structural constraints in which we live. To answer this question we also need to explore how gender is 'managed' by individuals in relation to other descriptors such as social class, age, nationality, ethnicity, race and so on.

Many analyses have explored ways in which individuals practice identities in different contexts, arguing that this varied practice creates conflict within the individual desperate to maintain a stable identity. For instance, the gay man who acts 'straight' at work in order not to experience discrimination does this at a cost: he experiences conflict and anxiety from this disjunctive identity. Recall in Chapter Two that analyses suggest that individuals usually attempt to assimilate, compartmentalize or ignore the disjunctures in performances, which silences diversity. From a postmodern perspective, however, the conflict resulting from diverse performances is inevitable and need not be interpreted negatively. Tension and conflict are productive in the Foucauldian (1980) sense in that the only option is not the silencing of particular parts, but that the outcome remains, indeed, uncertain. Tension and confrontation, are, in themselves, necessarily productive. Furthermore, tension can produce a change in the 'parts' themselves, affording a dynamic transformation. This is not to suppose that the product of negotiation will be positive, nor that the process will necessarily be experienced as liberating. What might be said is that the 'unity required for effective action does not require homogeneity' (Mullin, 1995: 28).

Scholarly literature in gender reveals an, as yet, fairly uneasy reaction to notions of difference. A focus on local narratives and recognition of differences between descriptors fits well with recent attempts to locate women and men within violent relationships. A number of feminist scholars have recently explored some implications of differences within descriptors. These include Haraway's (1989) critique of the foundational discourses of science as well as the works of Alcoff (1988), Hooks (1989), Butler (1992), Fraser and Nicholson (1988, 1994) and, Seidman (1997) on difference and identity politics.

The idea that identity is malleable raises questions concerning the degree to which individuals are 'free' to choose and perform their identities versus the degree to which performance is defined and constrained by societal structures. Although recent theory emphasizes the idea that gender does not signify static categories, we might still suggest that men and women are assigned a narrow field of attributes and attitudes. Moreover, it seems to be a fundamental condition of self-knowledge (that is, understanding one's own identity), that women and men both comprehend and accept these bifurcated characteristics (O'Neill and Hird, 2001). This comprehension is, though, predicated on a constant reflection with gender. Precisely because gender is neither immutable nor static, women and men are obliged to constantly reflect upon femininities and masculinities. Connell defines the relationship between the social actor and gender as a societal symbol:

> Meaning does not inhere in symbols, but must be invested in and interpreted from symbols by acting social being. Interpretation is the product of a series of associations, convergences and condensations established through praxis, and not the result of an act of decoding by the observer (1991, p.74).

Structure does provide boundaries which impinge on most individuals. The closer any individual gets to a particular boundary, the greater that individual will experience the constraints of these societal structures. But gender, as all other symbols involved with identity must be interpreted; even on a superficial level this interpretation requires a social actor. As Brittan writes, 'men are not simply the passive embodiments of the masculine ideology' (1989: 68).

## Heterosexual Interpersonal Violence

Although we talk about interpersonal violence as though it were a phenomenon; it is, in fact, human action (Kappeler, 1995). Interpersonal violence is configured and inscribed within a set of discourses, particularly those concerned with gender, identity and relationships. Those descriptors which are most obviously inscribed on our bodies are gender, age, social class, ethnicity and race; and are invoked to account for variances in interpersonal violence. Gender, as an element of identity, remains one of the most frequently invoked signifiers of personal violence, as well as a wide variety of abilities, sexuality, sex and family life. Many books, articles and television programs popularize the message that men and women are ultimately different and that the difference is self-evident, natural and immutable.

These gestures towards biology also allow the mechanisms through which small biological differences between females and males transform into large differentially prescribed personality traits to remain unspecified. The effect of ascribing differentiated personality traits to males and females *a priori* is to ignore or re-interpret any indications of gender 'transgressions'. The violent acts of women are re-constructed so that she becomes 'deviant' or a victim of men's violence. Non-aggressive men are similarly discursively re-constructed to become a 'sissy' or 'poofter'. This constant recourse to biological determinism ensures that both men and women's violent behavior is exonerated, increasing the likelihood that violent behavior will continue (Smart, 1976).

Interpersonal violence is closely bound up with gendered identity. Masculinity, in particular, has been historically associated with the maintenance of identity stasis through the use of violent action. What appears to be biological programming is in fact a complicated configuration of identity, learned and practiced over a lifetime. Research findings explored in Chapters Three and Four suggest that male children and adolescents expend a great deal of time in observing and practicing various behaviors, each of which related to already established gender markers.

Moreover, since dominant discourses maintain heteronormativity, all individuals can access this discourse to reinforce traditional gender practices. The positioning of most masculinities above femininities necessitates not only a false dichotomization but a fragile and tenuous hegemony. Every masculine identity that is based on assumptions that women are less intelligent, less strong, less adventurous, less competent, less persistent, less innovative, less rational, less 'masculine' are bound to be threatened on a regular basis be examples of women who are *more* of all of these qualities. It may be a wife who can carry her small children and the groceries without assistance, balance the check book, work full-time outside and inside the home, work out the answers to Jeopardy, read faster or maintain close friendships. Or it may be a girl who does better in school than her brother or boyfriend. When femininity gets too close to masculinity, violent action, which is already an *a priori* 'property' of male identity, may be used in an attempt to re-secure gender boundaries. At the same time that the violent action of men towards women in personal relationships maintains gender boundaries, it also reflects the imperfection of the gender order.

Indeed, the fragility of the gender order is powerfully revealed in our everyday language of the 'opposite' gender. This language sustains a dichotomy of 'us' and 'them', where 'they' are strangers:

> If the strangers are the people who do not fit the cognitive, moral, or aesthetic map of the world—one of these maps, two or all three; if they, therefore, by their sheer presence, make obscure what ought to be transparent, confuse what out to be a straightforward recipe for action, and/or prevent the satisfaction from being fully satisfying; if they pollute the joy with anxiety while making the forbidden fruit alluring; if, in other words, they befog and eclipse the boundary lines which ought to be clearly seen; if, having done all this, they gestate uncertainty, which in turn breeds the discomfort of feeling lost—then each society produces such strangers (Bauman, 1997, p.17).

Since gender boundaries are artificial, individuals are necessarily faced with constant gender transgressions. To deal with the anxiety (and indeed the forbidden fruit of 'other' gender practices), we create strangers out of the 'other' gender (as in 'men are from Mars, women are from Venus). Thus, hegemonic masculinity is not only threatened by the abilities of girls and women. Violence committed by two male schoolmates in the playground or two male friends in a bar may be understood as both a way of practicing a form of masculinity and of attempting to re-establish each male's identity investment. Violent behavior is about gendered identity but it is also about investment in identity. This investment is strongest in intimate relationships; the more intimate, the greater the vulnerability of each person and the greater the opportunity for each individual to detect this vulnerability. This can be especially true of gay and lesbian relationships which are often kept secret in order to avoid homophobic violence. Gay and lesbian relationships often carry this triple burden. The expectation of any intimate relationship, the burden of secrecy and the added burden that gay and lesbian relationships must somehow provide a more authentic relationship than the heterosexual, patriarchal one.

Thus, interpersonal relationships are the site at which identity investment and crisis are most likely to take place. The appropriateness of relationships as the context of identity negotiation is rarely contested. Indeed, there is an expectation that investment increases as the intimacy of the relationship increases. As the previous section relates, relationships are often understood in terms of rights and obligations; a contract of sorts. The idealization of the intimate relationship and the family in our society has produced a legacy of unfulfilled expectations. We enter relationships already fragile from years of identity performance and crises because our identities are predicated on false dichotomizations. We have different conceptions of what the ideal family, intimate relationships and friendships constitute which necessitates an inevitable negotiation: we also have different understandings of what negotiation is and how we should negotiate our needs, rights and obligations.

Marital and familial relationships enjoy a particular sanctified position in our society. Note the reluctance of communities to get involved in 'domestic disputes', precisely because the family is viewed as a private relationship. Individuals tend to acknowledge the destructive relationship only at the point at which its members become violent (Kappeler, 1995). This has the effect of legitimizing the violence in that it is the violence itself which seems to provide the impetus for individual and societal concern.

## Where to From Here?

Hegemony contributes to or constitutes a form of social cohesion not through force or coercion, nor necessarily through consent, but most effectively by way of practices, techniques, and methods which infiltrate minds and bodies, cultural practices which cultivate behaviors and beliefs, tastes, desires, and needs as seemingly naturally occurring qualities and properties embodied in the psychic and physical reality (or 'truth') of the human subject (Smart, 1995, p.210).

Any inquiry into a subject as important and emotive as heterosexual interpersonal violence has an interest in exploring possibilities for praxis. If interpersonal violence is about gendered identity crisis, then perhaps the solution lies in de-gendering society. That is, if the problem is gender, then the solution is androgyny. Radical feminist concerns with violence against women, and the Women's Movement of the 1960's and 1970's more generally, offered a powerful critique of this androgynization. This supposed deconstruction of gender actually meant a preferencing of 'male' subjectivity and the expectation that women's subjectivity approximate masculinity. This sameness-difference debate has effectively resulted in a stand-off.

More hopeful are recent emphases on deconstructionism within philosophy, sociology and political theory. A number of authors (Derrida, 1976; Foucault, 1984; Connell, 1987, 1990; Spelman, 1988; Grosz; 1989; Fraser, 1990; Hooks, 1990; Nicholson, 1990; Fausto-Sterling, 1992; Lorber, 1994; Weeks, 1995 and; Seidman, 1997 to name a few) are concerned to deconstruct the premises on which gender is constructed and maintained in society. These analyses offer insightful analyses of the ways in which masculinities and femininities are practiced within particular contexts. The recognition that gender does not really define a dichotomy but rather a large set of behaviors offers, paradoxically, both a reason for interpersonal violence and the possibility to challenge this violence. This text has shown how interpersonal violence can be understood as an action chosen by individuals to shore up or re-establish their gendered identities. The multiplicity of genders and the fragility which results from this multiplicity initiates crises in identity. But this multiplicity also opens up possibilities for reflexivity and change. To recognize that 'man' is not a homogenous, solid group is important because it suggests the possibility of internal divisions within this signifier. These internal divisions open up possibilities for individual men and women to take up different gender practices. At a group level it also offers the possibility of alliances between women and men who may not initially identify through gender but may identify commonalities around social class, age, ethnicity, race and so on. Whilst hegemonic masculinity has historically operated on the premise of preferencing gender concerns over others, it is equally possible for men and women to preference race or social class issues over gender.

I suspect that further calls for the deconstruction of gender will invite criticism on the grounds that deconstructionism produces nothing more than relativism and thus severely limits the possibility of political struggle.

What, after all, makes an individual part of a group is certainly some points of contact; a shared identity of some sort. This identity must include particularities in common with the group and differences with the larger social world. What makes some women identify as feminists, for example, is their particularity (that is 'woman') and difference from the larger group (women and men). But what defines any given particularity is precisely its relation to other particularities. When groups demand something (equal rights, more pay etc.) they refer to some universal principles, norms or values. When women and men fought for women's right to vote, it was an appeal to the universal principle of rights; hence 'universal' suffrage. Women could not claim that their absolute particularity deserved the right to vote but rather that their right to vote was predicated on women's shared identity with men as humans: women as equal to men. For any group asserting claims there seem to be two options: either define the group by its difference from society and remain outside the social relations or engage in a struggle between its particularity and the grounds for its universalism.

A focus on differences (race, class, gender, age, ethnicity, nationality and so on) appears at first glance to be irreconcilable with the politics of rights and justice. Put simply, if we identify ourselves by our differences, on what basis we are able to jockey for position in any community? Given that we define our differences through the differences of others, it follows that any fully differentiated individual or group would require a status quo in social relations (Laclau, 1995). But this is clearly not the case. The socio-political map is fraught with struggles between groups. As Anna Yeatman (1993) points out, what in fact does happen is a constant struggle between marginalization (in which groups define themselves primarily through their difference) and hybridization (where the group transcends its own identity in an attempt to change its location within the community). Further, the relationship between diversity and community is necessarily hegemonic because it consists of a constant struggle between two opposing, yet co-dependent needs. What we end up with is a negotiation, tenuous and fragile, between the particulars that form our shifting identities and the universal tenets through which we hope to achieve our demands. Moreover, the very fact of this tension makes political struggle tenuous and it is for this reason that analysis of the negotiation between difference and universal is most usefully defined in terms of 'moments'. This notion signifies both the tenuousness and indeterminacy of struggle.

Building on the notion that socio-political conflict is constituted by the tension between diversity and community, it might be more useful to formulate an understanding of the political field as resembling an empty site on which 'moments' of struggle are fought. That is, there is no *a priori* foundational ground. Rather, contemporary society 'constitutes a site, space, or clearing for political possibilities, rather than a distinctive political strategy' (Smart, 1993: 103). This differs from other conceptions that contemporary society is reaching towards emancipation as its ultimate project. Feminist scholars have shown that what constitutes societal emancipation has actually been an attempt to articulate a universal, male, Western voice of reason. The indeterminacy of the ground beyond the difference-community struggle, often called the 'postmodern imagination' has been viewed as either irritatingly absent of political agenda or a form of conservative politics (Habermas, 1981; Callinicos, 1989). However, an alternative interpretation suggests that contemporary debates extend the site of political possibilities. At the very least they invite us to reconsider modern reason from a new approach to subjectivity, one which sees the subject as the fragmented negotiation of struggle between difference and community:

> ...subjectivity is no longer assigned to the apolitical wasteland of essences and essentialism. Subjectivity is now read as multiple, layered, and non-unitary; rather than being constituted in a unified and integrated ego, the 'self' is seen as being 'constituted out of and by difference and remains contradictory (Giroux, 1991, p.30).

Solidarity is presumed to be a necessary pre-cursor to successful community organization, particularly if that community is involved in some sort of political struggle. In the case of a group of individuals, they may with little difficulty silence one of more individuals and indeed exclude those individuals who do not represent sufficient homogeneity with the group. This option is not available to the individual in negotiating her or his selves. As I have attempted to demonstrate, postmodern theory attempts to re-dress the suppression of differences in the call for political unity. However, we are left with the apparent danger of not being able to organize at all for political struggle. This danger is predicated on a particular understanding of social movement theory in which identities are already formed, are stable, and become visible through political organizing and struggle (Gamson, 1996). Postmodern theory, which emphasizes identity as unstable, fluid and constructed, invites a re-thinking of social movement theory which has tended to assume the existence of an established collective identity (Gamson, 1992). Most identity politics is both strategic (what works) and constitutive of a power struggle (who gets to say what women and men are). But it is more than these things: it is a struggle to identify who 'us' is, who 'we' are.

Social struggle concerned with ending heterosexual interpersonal violence is possible and there are many organizations that are currently involved in challenging the associated link between masculinity and aggression. Identity politics signals that there are a variety of political movements, some governed under the auspices of challenging bifurcated notions of gender and others dependent on this very essentialism. Generally, there has been a movement away from static notions of masculinity and femininity and this has opened spaces to understand personal violence in different ways. However, political organization of this sort, predicated on deconstructing links between gender and violence, must necessarily be involved in a constant process of negotiation. If our system of signification is predicated on bifurcation, then as one dichotomy is deconstructed and challenged this process will be resisted and challenged by other forms of dichotomization.

Attempts to challenge personal violence need to acknowledge the importance of gender, identity and relationships in configuring this form of violence. Most importantly we need to recognize that gender does not signify two homogenous groups: care in theorizing needs to be given to any investigations of the association between gender and violence so that we do not simply reproduce the 'nature of violence' as immutably gendered.

## Notes

1   Maccoby and Jacklin (1974) reviewed ninety studies measuring sex-related differences in aggression. According to their findings, between thirty-three percent and fifty percent of the these studies found no significant sex-related differences in human aggression. Between forty-six percent and sixty-one percent found males to be more aggressive and eight percent found that females were more aggressive.

2   For a comprehensive critique of personality scales see Lafitte's *The Personality in Psychology* (1957) and Connell's *Gender and Power* (1987).

3   It is possible to argue that the ultimate consequence of recent debates which emphasize the infinite shifting and temporary nature of gender is the erasure of the very concept of gender itself.

4   Others (such as O'Neill and Hird, 2001) refer to masculinities as located on a continuum with the dominant construct at one extreme and its antithesis, the effeminate homosexual, at the other.

# Bibliography

Ahmad, Y. Whitney, I. and Smith, P. (1991), 'A Survey Service for Schools on Bully/victim Problems', in P. Smith, and D. Thompson (eds), *Practical Approaches to Bullying*, David Fulton, London.

Alcoff, L. (1988), 'Cultural Feminism vs. Poststructuralism: The Identity Crisis in Feminist Theory', *Signs*, Vol. 13, pp.405-436.

Alcoff, L. and Potter, E. (1993), *Feminist Epistemologies*, Routledge, New York.

Allen, H. (1987), 'Rendering Them Harmless: The Professional Portrayal of Women Charged with Serious Violent Crimes', in P. Carlen and A. Worrall (eds), *Gender, Crime and Justice*, Open University Press, Milton Keynes.

Ardrey, R. (1967), *African Genesis*, Dell Publishers, New York.

Australian Bureau of Statistics (1995), *National Crime Statistics*.

Baker, P. (1992), 'Heterosexuality and Pornography', in K. Itzen (ed.) *Pornography*, Oxford University Press, Oxford.

Balthazar, M. and Cook, R. (1984), 'An Analysis of the Factors Related to the Rate of Violent Crimes Committed by Incarcerated Female Delinquents', in S. Chaneles (ed.) *Gender Issues, Sex Offences, and Criminal Justice*, The Haworth Press, New York.

Bandura, A. (1973), *Aggression: A Social Learning Analysis*. Englewood Cliffs, Prentice-Hall, New Jersey.

Bandura, A. and Waiters, R. (1963), *Social Learning and Personality Development*, Holt, Rinehart and Winston, New York.

Barnes, G., Greenwood, L. and Sommer, R. (1991), 'Courtship Violence in a Canadian Sample of Male College Students', *Family Relations*, Vol. 40, pp. 37-44.

Barrett, M. (1988), *Women's Oppression Today*, Verso, London.

Bateman, P. (1991), 'The Context of Date Rape', in B. Levy (ed.) *Dating Violence: Young Women in Danger*, Seal Press, Seattle, W A.

Beck, U. and Beck-Gemsheim, E. (1995), *The Normal Chaos of Love*, Polity Press, Oxford.

Berger, M., Wallis, B. and Watson, S. (eds) (1995) *Constructing Masculinity*, Routledge, New York.

Boulton, M. and Underwood, K. (1992), 'Bully/victim Problems Among Middle School Children', *British Journal of Educational Psychology*, Vol. 62, pp. 73-97.

Bourdieu, P. (1977), *Outline of a Theory of Practice*. Translation R. Nice, Cambridge University Press, Cambridge.

Braidotti, R. (1994), *Nomadic Subjects: Embodiment and Sexual Difference in Contemporary Feminist Theory*, Columbia University Press, New York.

Branwhite, T. (1994), 'Bullying and Student Distress: Beneath the Tip of the Iceberg', *Educational Psychology*, Vol. 14, pp. 59-71.

Breines, W. and Gordon, L. (1983), 'The New Scholarship on Family Violence', *Signs: Journal of Women in Culture and Society*, Vol. 8, pp. 491-453.

Brittan, A. (1989), *Masculinity and Power*, Blackwell, Oxford.

Brownmiller, S. (1975), *Against Our Will. Men, Women and Rape*, Simon and Schuster, New York.

Bula, F. (1992), 'Teenage Girls Learn About Abuse', *The Montreal Gazette*, 1 June, pp. Cl,C4.

Burcky, W., Reuterman, N. and Kopsky, S. (1988), 'Dating Violence Among High School Students', The *School Counsellor*, Vol. 35, pp. 353-359.

Burt, M. and Albin, R. (1981), 'Rape Myths, Rape Definitions, and Probability of Conviction', *Journalof Applied Social Psychology*, Vol. 11, pp. 212-230.

Butler, J. (1990), *Gender Trouble*, Routledge, London.

Butler, J. (1993), *Bodies that Matter. On the Discursive Limits of 'Sex'*, Routledge, London.

Butler, J. and Scott, J. (ed.) (1992), *Feminists Theorize the Political*, Routledge, New York.

Callaghan, S. and Joseph, S. (1995), *Personal Individual Differences*, Vol. 18, pp. 161-163.

Callinicos, A. (1989), *Against Postmodernism: A Marxist Critique*, Polity Press, Cambridge.

Cameron, D. and Frazer, E. (1994), 'Cultural Difference and the Lust to Kill', in P. Harvey and P. Gow (eds) *Sex and Violence*, Routledge, London.

Cameron, D. and Frazer, E. (1994), 'Masculinity, Violence and Sexual Murder', in *The Polity Reader in Gender Studies*, Polity Press, Oxford.

Campbell, A. (1993), *Out of Control. Men, Women and Aggression*, Pandora, London.

Chesney-Lind, M. (1973), 'Judicial Enforcement of the Female Sex Role: The Family Court and the Female Delinquent', *Issues in Criminology*, Vol. 8, pp. 51-69.

Chesney-Lind, M. (1986), 'Women and Crime: The Female Offender', *Signs*, Vol. 12, pp. 78-96.

Chodorow, N. (1978), *The Reproduction of Mothering*, University of California Press, California.

Chodorow, N. (1989), *Feminism and Psychoanalytic Theory*, Polity Press, Oxford.

Coie, J. el al. (1991), 'The Role of Aggression in Peer Relations: An Analysis of Aggression Episodes in Boys' Play Groups', *Child Development*, Vol. 62, pp. 812-826.

Comstock, G. (1991), 'Television Violence and Antisocial Behavior and Aggressive Behavior', in M. Miedzian *Boys Will Be Boys*, Virago, London.

Connell, R. (1987), *Gender and Power*, Polity Press, Oxford.

Connell, R. (1995), *Masculinities*, Polity Press, Oxford.

Constantinople, A. (1973), 'Masculinity - Femininity: An Exception to a Famous Dictum, *Psychological Bulletin*, pp. 80.

Cornell, D. (1992), *The Philosophy of the Limit*, Routledge, New York.

Cowie, J., Cowie, V. and Slater, E. (1968), *Delinquency in Girls*, Heinemann, London.

Daly, M. (1978), *Gyn/Ecology*, The Women's Press, London.

Daly, M. and Wilson, M. (1988), *Homicide*, Aldine de Gruyter, New York.

Darwin, C. (1859), *The Origin of Species*, John Murray, London.

Dawkins, R. (1989), *The Selfish Gene*. Second Edition, Oxford University Press, Oxford.

DeBeauvoir, S. (1953), *The Second Sex*, Penguin, Middlesex.

DeKeseredy, W. (1988), *Woman Abuse in Dating Relationships: The Role of Male Peer Support*, Canadian Scholars' Press Inc., Toronto.

Delphy, C. (1994), 'Changing Women in a Changing Europe. Is 'Difference' the Future for Feminism?', *Women's Studies International Forum*, Vol. 17, pp. 187-201.

Derrida, J. (1976), *Of Grammatology*, The Johns Hopkins University Press, Baltimore.

Derrida, J. (1978), *Writing and Difference*. Translation by A. Bass, University of Chicago Press, Chicago.

Dobash, R.E. and Dobash R. (1979), *Violence Against Wives: A Case Against Patriarchy*, Free Press, New York.

Dobash, R.E., Dobash R. and Noaks, L. (eds) (1995), *Gender and Crime*, University of Wales Press, Cardiff.

Dobash, R.E., Dobsash, R., Wilson, M. and Daly, M. (1992), 'The Myth of Sexual Symmetry in Marital Violence', *Social Problems*, Vol. 39, pp. 71-91.

Dodge, K., Price, J., Coie, J. and Christopoulos, C. (1990), 'On the Development of Aggressive Dyadic Relationships in Boys' Peer Groups', *Human Development*, Vol. 33, pp. 260-270.

Donnerstein E., Linz, D. and Penrod, S. (1987), *The Question of Pornography: Research Findings and Policy Implications*, The Free Press, New York.

Doyle, A., Connolly, J. and Rivest, L. (1980), 'The Effect of Playmate Familiarity on the Social Interaction of Young Children', *Child Development*, Vol. 51, pp. 217-223.

Drouet, D. (1993), 'Adolecent Female Bullying and Sexual Harassment', in D. Tattum *Understanding and Managing Bullying*, Heinemann Educational Books Ltd., Oxford.

Durkheim, E. (1933), *The Division of Labour in Society*, The Free Press, New York.

Durrenberger, D. (1993), 'Statements on Introduced Bills and Joint Resolutions', *Congressional Record*. 12 May.

Dworkin, A. (1987), *Intercourse*, Arrow Books, London.

Ehrenreich, B. and English, D. (1979), *For Her Own Good*, Doubleday, New York.

Eisler, R. (1996), *Sacred Pleasure*, Harper, San Francisco.

Elliott, F.A. (1976), 'The Neurology of Explosive Rage. The Dyscontrol Syndrome', *Practioner*, Vol. 217, pp. 51-60.

Ellis, L. (1989), *Theories of Rape: Inquiries into the Causes of Sexual Aggression*, Hemisphere Publishing Corporation, New York.

Erikson, E. (1951), *Childhood and Society*, Imago Publishing, London.

Ewing, C. (1997), *Fatal Families. The Dynamics of Intrafamilial Homicide*, Sage, Thousand Oaks.

Faludi, S. 1992: *Backlash: The Undeclared War Against Women*, Chattod Windus, London.

Fausto-Sterling, A. (1992), *Myths of Gender. Biological Theories about Women and Men*. Second Edition, Basic Books, New York.

Farrell, W. (1993), *Why Men Are The Way They Are*, McGraw-Hill, New York.

FBI Supplementary Homicide Report (1996), in A. Dobrin; B. Wiersema; C. Loftin and D. McDowall (eds), *Statistical Handbook of Violence in America*, Oryx Press, Phoenix.

Fedigan, L. (1982), *Primate Paradigms*, Eden, Montreal.

Feinstein, D. (1993), 'The Crime Bill', *Congressional Record*, 3 November: S14923-14926.

Fine, M. (1988), 'Sexuality, Schooling and Adolescent Females: The Missing Discourse of Desire', *Harvard Educational Review*, Vol. 58, pp. 29-53.

Firestone, S. (1970), *The Dialectic of Sex*, The Women's Press, London.

Flax, J. (1987), 'Postmodemism and Gender Relations in Feminist Theory', *Signs: Journal of Women in Culture and Society*, Vol. 12, pp. 621-643.

Follinstad, D., Wright, S., Lloyd, S. and Sebastian, J. (1991), 'Sex Differences in Motivations and Effects in Dating Violence', *Family Relations*, Vol. 40, pp. 51-57.

Foucault, M. (1965), *Madness and Civilization*, Penguin, London.

Foucault, M. (1973), *The Order of Things*, Vintage Books, New York.

Foucault, M. (1979), *Discipline and Punish*, Penguin, London.

Foucault, M. (1982), 'The Subject and Power', in H. Dreyfus and P. Rabinow (eds) *Michel Foucault, Beyond Structuralism and Hermeneutics*, University of Chicago Press, Chicago.

Fraser, N. and Nicholson, L. (1994), 'Social Criticism Without Philosophy: An Encounter Between Feminism and Postmodemism' in S. Seidman (ed.) *The Postmodern Turn*, Cambridge University Press, Cambridge.

French, M. (1985), *Beyond Power: On Women, Men and Morals*, Cardinal, London.

Freud, S. (1901), 'Three Essays on the Theory of Sexuality', in *The Standard Edition of the Complete Psychological Works of Sigmund Freud, Vol. VII*, Translated by J. Strachey with A. Freud, The Hogarth Press, London.

Freud, S. (1931), 'Female Sexuality', in *The Standard Edition of the Complete Psychological Works of Sigmund Freud, Vol. XXI*, Translated by J. Strachey with A. Freud, The Hogarth Press, London.

Frude, N. (1991), *Understanding Family Problems: A Psychological Approach*, John Wiley and Sons, Chichester.

Frye, M. (1983), *The Politics of Reality: Essays in Feminist Theory*, Crossing Press, Trumansburg, New York.

Fuss, D. (1989), *Essentially Speaking. Feminism, Nature and Difference*, Routledge, London.

Gamson, W. (1992), 'The Social Psychology of Collective Action', in A. Morris and C. Mueller (eds), *Frontiers in Social Movement Theory*, Yale University Press, New Haven.

Gamson, I. (1996), 'Must Identity Politics Self-destruct? A Queer Dilemma', in S. Seidman (ed), *Queer Theory/Sociology*, Blackwell, Oxford.

Gavey, N. (1996), 'Women's Desire and Sexual Violence Discourse', in S. Wilkinson (ed.), *Feminist Social Psychologies*, Open University Press, Buckingham.

Gayford, I. (1975), 'Wife Battering: A Preliminary Survey of 100 Cases', *British Medical Journal*, Vol. 1, pp. 194-197.

Gelles, R. (1977), 'Abused Wives: Why Do They Stay?', *Journal of Marriage and the Family*, Vol. 38, pp. 659-668.

Gelles, R. and Straus, M.A. (1988), *Intimate Violence: The Causes and Consequences of Abuse in the American Family*, Touchstone: Simon and Schuster, New York.

Gibbs, N. (1993), 'Cover Story: Till Death Do Us Part', *Time*, Vol. 141, pp. 38-45.

Glueck, S. and Glueck. E. (1934), *One Thousand Juvenile Delinquents: Their Treatment By Court and Clinic*, Harvard University Press, Cambridge, MA.

Giroux, H. (ed.) (1991), *Postmodernism, Feminism and Cultural Politics*, State University of New York Press, New York.

Goldner, V., Penn, P., Sheinber, M. and Walker, G. (1990), 'Love and Violence: Gender Paradoxes in Volatile Attachments', *Family Process*, Vol. 29, pp. 343-364.

Goodenough, R. (1987), 'Small Group Culture and the Emergence of Sexist Behavior: A Comparative Study of Four Children's Groups', in G. Spinder and L. Spindler (eds), *Interpretive Ethnography in Education: At Home and Abroad*, Lawrence Erlbaum Associates Publishers, London.

Gordon, C. (1991), 'Governmental Rationalities', in G. Burchell, C. Gordon and P. Miller (eds), *The Foucault Effect: Studies on Governmentality*, Chicago University Press, Chicago.

Government Statistical Service, HMSO. (1994), *Criminal Statistics England and Wales 1994*, HMSO, London.

Gramsci, A. (1971), *Selections From the Prison Notebooks*, International Publishers, New York.

Grant, L. (1984), 'Gender Roles and Statuses in School Children's Peer Interactions', *Sociological Review*, Vol. 14, pp. 58- 76.

Grosz, E. (1989), *Sexual Subversions. Three French Feminists*, Allen and Unwin, St. Leonards.

Grosz, E. (1994), *Volatile Bodies*, Indiana University Press, Bloomington.

Groth, A. and Brinbaum, H. (1979), *Men Who Rape: The Psychology of the Offender*, Plenum, New York.

Gryl, R., Smith, S. and Bird, G. (1991), 'Close Dating Relationships Among College Students: Differences by Use of Violence and by Gender', *Journal of Social and Personal Relationships*, Vol. 8, pp. 243-264.

Guardian, The (1996), 'Woman Under Protection Was Raped by Stalker', *The Guardian*, January 30, p. 2.

Habermas, J. (1981), *The Theory of Communicative Action. Vol.1*, Polity Press, Oxford.

Haraway, D. (1989), *Primate Visions: Gender, Race, and Nature in the World of Modern Science*, Routledge, New York.

Haraway, D. (1990), 'A Manifesto For Cyborgs: Science, Technology, and Socialist Feminism in the 1980s', in L. Nicholson (ed.), *Feminism/Postmodernism*, Routledge, London.

Harding, S. (1987), *Feminism and Methodology*, Open University Press, Milton Keynes.

Harstock, N. (1983), 'Difference and Domination in the Women's Movement: The Dialect of Theory and Practice', in A. Swerdlow and H. Lesinger (eds), *Class, Race and Sex: The Dynamics of Control*, G.K. Hall, Boston.

Heidensohn, P. (1995), *Women and Crime*, New York University Press, New York.

Henton, J., Cate, R., Koval, J., Lloyd, S. and Christopher, S. (1983), 'Romance and Violence in Dating Relationships', *Journal of Family Issues*, Vol. 4, pp. 467-482.

Herbert, C. (1989), *Talking of Silence: The Sexual Harassment of Schoolgirls*, The Palmer Press, Sussex.

Hilberman and Munson (1977), 'Sixty Battered Women', *Victimology*, Vols. 3-4, pp. 460-462.

Hird, M. (1995a), 'Adolescent Dating Violence: An Empirical Study', *Intervention*, Vol. 100, pp. 60-69.

Hird, M. (1995b), *Adolescent Dating Violence and the Negotiation of Gender*. Unpublished Thesis. Oxford University.

Hird, M. (1998), 'Theorising Pupil Identity As Fragmented: Some Implications For Feminist Critical Pedagogy', *British Journal of Sociology of Education*, Vol. 19, pp. 517 -527.

Hird, M. (2000a), 'An Empirical Study of Adolescent Dating Aggression in the UK', *Journal of Adolescence*, Vol.23, pp. 69-78.

Hird, M. (2000b), 'Gender's Nature: Intersexuality, Transsexualism and the 'Sex'/'Gender' Binary, *Feminist Theory*, Vol.1, pp. 347-364.

Hird, M. and Jackson, S. (2001), 'Where 'Angels' and 'Wooses' Fear to Tread: Sexual Coercion in Adolescent Heterosexual Dating Relationships', *Australian and New Zealand Journal of Sociology*, Vol.37, pp. 27-43.

HMSO (1989), *Discipline in Schools: Report of the Committee of Enquiry* Chaired by Lord Elton, HMSO, London.

Hofeller, K. (1982), *Social, Psychological and Situational Factors in Wife Abuse*, R & E Research Associates, Palo Alto.

Holland, J., Ramazanoglu, C. and Thomson, R. (1996), 'In The Same Boat? The Gendered (In)experience of First Heterosex', in D. Richardson (ed.), *Theorising Heterosexuality*, Open University Press, Buckingham.

Holland, J., Ramazanoglu, C., Sharpe, S. and Thomson, R. (1996), 'Reputations: Journeying Into Gendered Power Relations', in J. Weeks and J. Holland (eds), *Sexual Cultures, Communities, Values and Intimacy*, Macmillan, London.

Hollway, W. (1984), 'Gender Difference and the Production of Subjectivity', in U. Henriques and Walkerdine (eds), *Changing the Subject*, Methuen, London.

Hollway, W. (1989), *Subjectivity and Method in Psychology*, Sage, London.

Hollway, W. (1995), 'Feminist Discourses and Women's Heteroseuxal Desire', in S. Wilkinson and C. Kitzinger (eds), *Feminism and Discourse. Psychological Perspectives*, Sage, London.

Hooks, B. (1990), 'Postmodem Blackness', *Postmodern Culture*, Vol. 1, pp. 1-15.

Horsfall, J. (1991), *The Presence of the Past: Male Violence in the Family*, Allen and Unwin, Sydney.

Huyssen, A. (1984), 'Mapping the Postmodem', *New German Critique*, Vol. 33, pp. 5-52.

Hyde, J. (1990), 'Meta-analysis and the Psychology of Gender Differences', *Signs: Journal of Women in Culture and Society*, Vol. 16, pp. 55- 73.

Irigaray, L. (1985a), *This Sex Which is Not One*, Cornell University Press, Ithaca.

Irigaray, L. (1985b), *Speculum of the Other Woman*, Cornell University Press, Ithaca.

Jacobs, P. et al. (1965), 'Aggressive Behavior, Mental Abnormality and the XYY Male', *Nature*, Vol. 208, pp. 1351-1352.

Jamieson, L. (1998), *Intimacy. Personal Relationships in Modern Societies*, Polity Press, Oxford.

Jenny, C. (1988), 'Adolescent Risk-taking Behavior and the Occurrence of Sexual Assault', *American Journal of Diseases of Children*, Vol. 142, pp. 770- 772.

Jones, A. (1991), *Women Who Kill*, Victor Gollancz, London.

Jukes, A. (1993), *Why Men Hate Women*, Free Association Books, London.

Jung, C. (1953), 'The Relations Between the Ego and the Unconscious', *Collected Work, volume 7: Two Essays on Analytical Psychology*, Routledge and Kegan Paul, London.

Kappeler, S. (1995), *The Will to Power*, Polity Press, Oxford.

Kelly, L. (1984), 'Some Thoughts on Feminist Experience in Research on Male Sexual Violence', *Studies in Sexual Politics*, Vol. 2, pp. 61-88.

Kelly, L. (1987), 'The Continuum of Sexual Violence', in J. Hanmer and M. Maynard (eds), *Women, Violence and Social Control*, Macmillan, London.

Kelly, L. (1988), *Surviving Sexual Violence*, Polity Press, Cambridge.

Kelly, L. (1992), 'Outrageous Injustice', *Community Care Supplement*, Vol. 25, pp. ii-iii.

Kennedy Bergen, R. (1995), 'Surviving Wife Rape. How Women Define and Cope With the Violence', *Violence Against Women*, Vol. 1, pp. 362-382.

Kimmel, M. (1997), 'Masculinity as Homophobia: Fear, Shame, and Silence in the Construction of Gender Identity', in M. Gergen and S. Davis (eds), *Toward a New Psychology of Gender*, Routledge, London.

Kirby, V. (1997), *Telling Flesh*, Routledge, New York.

Kolata, G. (1976), Primate Behavior: Sex and the Dominant Male', *Science*, Vol. 191, pp. 55-56.

Konopka, G. (1966), *The Adolescent Girl in Conflict*, Prentice-Hall, Englewood Cliffs, New Jersey.

Kuhl, (1982), 'Community Responses to Battered Women', *Victimology*, Vol. 7, pp. 49-52.

Kutner, L. (1991), 'Teenage Girls Endure Abusive Relationships', *The Montreal Gazette*.

Lacan, J. (1977), *The Four Fundamental Concepts of Psycho-analysis*. Translation by Alan Sheridan, Penguin, London.

Laclau, E. (1995), 'Subject of Politics, Politics of the Subject', *Differences: A Journal of Feminist Cultural Studies*, Vol. 7, pp. 157-166.

Lafitte, P. (1957), *The Person in Psychology: Reality or Abstraction*, Routledge and Kegan Paul, London.

Lees, S. (1993), *Sugar and Spice*, Penguin, London.

Leonard, E. (1982), *Women, Crime and Society. A Critique of Criminological Theory*, Longman, New York.

Levy, B. (1991), 'Support Groups: Empowerment For Young Women Abused in Dating Relationships', in B. Levy (ed.), *Dating Violence. Young Women in Danger*, The Seal Press, Seattle.

Lloyd, S. (1991), 'The Darkside of Courtship: Aggression and Sexual Exploitation', *Family Relations*, Vol. 40, pp. 14-20.

Lloyd, A. (1995), *Doubly Deviant, Doubly Damned*, Penguin, London.

Lobel, K. (1986), *Naming the Violence*, The Seal Press, Seattle.

Lombroso, C. and Ferrero, W. (1895), *The Female Offender*, Fisher Unwin, London.

Lorber, J. (1994), *Paradoxes of Gender*, Yale University Press, New Haven.

Lorenz, C. (1966), *On Aggression*, Methuen, London.

Lupri, E. (1990), 'Male Violence in the Home', in C. McKie and K. Thompson (eds), *Canadian Social Trends*, Thompson Educational Publishing, Toronto.

Lyotard, J. (1984), *The Postmodern Condition*, University of Minnesota, Minneapolis.

Maccoby, E. and Jacklin, C. (1974), *The Psychology of Sex Differences*, Stanford University Press, Stanford.

Mac An Ghaill, M. (1996), *Understanding Masculinities*, Open University Press, Buckingham.

MacKinnon, C. (1987), *Feminism and the Power of Law*, Harvard University Press, Cambridge.

Mahoney, P. (1985), *Schools for the Boys*, Hutchinson, London.

Makepeace, J. (1981), 'Courtship Violence Among College Students', *Family Relations*, Vol. 30, pp. 97-102.

McCarl Nielsen, J. (1990), *Feminist Research Methods*, Westview Press, Boulder.

Mead, G. (1962), *Mind, Self, and Society*, University of Chicago Press, Chicago.

Mercer, S. (1986), 'Not a Pretty Picture: An Exploratory Study of Violence Against Women in High School Dating Relationships', *Resources For Feminist Research*, Vol. 17, pp. 15-23.

Miedzian, M. (1991), *Boys Will Be Boys*, Virago, London.

Mill, J. (1987), *An Examination of Sir William Hamilton's Philosophy*, Longmans, Green, Reader and Dyer, Longond.

Millett, K. (1969), *Sexual Politics*, Virago Press, London.

Mills, T. (1985), 'The Assault on the Self: Stages in Coping With Battering Husbands', *Qualitative Sociology*, Vol. 8, pp. 103-123.

Money, J. and Ehrhardt, A. (1972), *Man and Woman, Boy and Girl*, Johns Hopkins University Press, Baltimore.

Moore, H. (1994), *A Passion For Difference*, Polity Press, Oxford.

Morris, A. (1987), *Women, Crime and Criminal Justice*, Blackwell, Oxford.

Morris, A. and Wilczynski, A. (1993), 'Rocking the Cradle: Mothers Who Kill Their Children' in H. Birch (ed.), *Moving Targets. Women, Murder and Representation*, Virago Press, London.

Morrison, T. et al. (1997), 'Gender Stereotyping, Homonegativity, and Misconception About Sexually Coercive Behavior Among Adolescents', *Youth and Society*, Vol. 28, pp. 351-364.

Moseley-Braun, C. (1993a), 'Senate Concurrent Resolution 21- Relative to Domestic Violence and Battered Women', *Congressional Record*, 30 March.

Moseley-Braun, C. (1993b), 'Violent Crime Control and Law Enforcement Act of 1993', *Congressional Record*, 9 November.

Muehlenhard, C. (1988), 'Misinterpreted Dating Behavior and the Risk of Date Rape', *Journal of Social And Clinical Psychology*, Vol. 6, pp. 20-37.

Muehlenhard, C. and Linton, M. (1987), 'Date Rape and Sexual Aggression in Dating Situations: Incidence and Risk Factors', *Journal of Counselling Psychology*, Vol. 34, pp. 186-196.

Mullin, A. (1995), 'Selves, Diverse and Divided: Can Feminists Have Diversity Without Multiplicity?', *Hypatia*, Vol. 10, pp. 1-30.

Naffin, N. (1985), 'The Masculinity-Femininity Hypothesis: A Consideration of Gender-based Personality Theories of Female Crime', *British Journal of Criminology*, Vol. 25, pp. 365-381.

Namaste, K. (1996), 'The Politics of Inside/Out: Queer Theory, Postructuralism, and a Sociological Approach to Sexuality', in S. Seidman (ed.), *Queer Theory/Sociology*. Blackwell, London.

Newbum, T. and Stanko, E. (1994), *Just Boys Doing Business?: Men, Masculinities and Crime*, Routledge, London.

*New Zealand Herald* (1997), 'Murder Sentencing Options Planned', January 13, pp. A3.

NiCarthy, G. (1991), 'Addictive Love and Abuse: A Course for Teenage Women', in B. Levy (ed.), *Dating Violence. Young Women in Danger*, The Seal Press, Seattle.

Nicholson, L. (1990), *Feminism/Postmodernism*, Routledge, London.

Nietzsche, F. (1968), *The Will to Power*, Vintage, New York.

Oakley, A. (1974), *The Sociology of Housework*, Martin Robertson, Bath.

Oakley, A. (1986), *From Here to Maternity*, Penguin, Harmondsworth.

O'Keeffe, N., Brockopp, K. and Chew, E. (1986), 'Teen Dating Violence', *Social Work*, Vol. 31, pp. 465-468.

O'Moore, A. and Hillery, B. (1989), 'Bullying in Dublin Schools', *The Irish Journal of Psychology*, Vol. 10, pp. 426-441.

O'Neill, T. and Hird, M. (2001), 'Double Damnation: Disabled Men and the Negotiation of Masculinity' in K. Backett-Milburn and L. McKie (eds), *Constructing Gendered Bodies*, Palgrave, London

Olweus, D. (1993), *Bullying at School*, Blackwell, Oxford.

Ostriker, A. (1986), *Stealing the Language: The Emergence of Women 's Poetry in America*, Beacon Press, Boston.

Oswald, H. et al. (1987), 'Gaps and Bridges: Interactions Between Girls and Boys in Elementary School', in P. Adler and P. Adler (eds.), *Sociological Studies of Child Development. Vol.2*, JAI Press, Grennwich.

Perry, D., Lusel, S. and Perry, L. (1988), 'Victims of Peer Aggression', *Developmental Psychology*, Vol. 24, pp. 807-814.

Pollak, O. (1950), *The Criminality of Women*, University of Pennsylvania Press, Pennsylvania.

Polk, K. (1994), *When Men Kill. Scenarios of Masculine Violence*, Cambridge University Press, Cambridge.

Renzetti, C. (1992), *Violent Betrayal*, Sage, Newbury Park.

Resnick, H. et al. (1991), 'Marital Rape', in R. Amrnerman and M. Merson (eds), *Case Studies in Family Violence*, Plenum, New York.

Rhode, D. (1990), *Theoretical Perspectives on Sexual Difference*, Yale University Press, New Haven.

Rich, A. (1986), *Of Woman Born*, W.W. Norton and Company, New York.

Richardson, D. (1996), *Theorizing Heterosexuality*, Open University Press, Buckingham.

Roberts, D. (1995), 'Motherhood and Crime', *Social Text*, Vol. 42, pp. 99-123.

Roberts, H. (1981), *Doing Feminist Research*, Routledge and Kegan Paul, London.

Rose, N. (1996), *Inventing Our Selves*, Cambridge University Press, Cambridge.

Rose, R., Gordon, T. and Bemstein, I. (1972), 'Plasma Testosterone Levels in Male Rhesus: Influence of Sexual and Social Stimuli', *Science*, Vol. 178, pp. 643-645.

Rounsaville and Weissmann (1977), 'Battered Women: A Medical Problem Requiring Detection', *International Journal of Psychology*, Vol. 191.

Rowell, T. (1972), *Social Behavior of Monkeys*, Penguin: Harmondsworth.

Rowell, T. (1974), 'The Concept of Social Dominance', *Behavior Biology*, Vol. 11, pp. 131-154.

Rubin, G. (1993), 'Thinking Sex: Notes For a Radical Theory of the Politics of Sexuality', in H. Abelove, M. Barale and D. Halperin (eds), *The Lesbian and Gay Studies Reader*, Routledge, New York.

Ruddick, S. (1989), *Maternal Thinking: Toward a Politics of Peace*, Beacon Press, Boston.

Russell, D. (1982), *Rape in Marriage*, Macmillan, New York.

Sanday, P. (1981), *Female Power and Male Dominance*, Cambridge University Press, Cambridge.

Sartre, J. (1965), *Being and Nothingness*, Translation by Hazel Barnes, The Citadel Press, New York.

Schechter, S. (1982), *Women and Male Violence: The Visions and Struggles of the Battered Women's Movement*, South End Press, Boston.

Schenck, W. (1992), *Violence Against Women*, Committee on the Judiciary Hearing. U.S. House, Washington D.C., 6 February.

Schultz, L.G. (1960), 'The Wife Assaulter', *Corrective Psychiatry and Journal of Social Therapy*, Vol. 6, pp. 103-112.

Schumer, C. (1992), *Violence on Television*, U.S. House Committee on the Judiciary. Hearing. 15 December. Washington D.C.

Seidman, S. (1993), *The Postmodern Turn*, Cambridge University Press, Cambridge.

Seidman, S. (1996), *Queer Theory/Sociology*, Blackwell, Oxford.

Segal, L. (1990), *Slow Motion*, Rutgers University Press, New Brunswick.

Shaw, M. (1995), 'Conceptualizing Violence By Women', in R.E. Dobash, R. Dobash and L. Noaks (eds), *Gender and Crime*, University of Wales Press, Cardiff.

Simon, R. (1975), *Women and Crime*, Lexington Books, Lexington.

Slee, P. (1993), 'Bullying: A Preliminary Investigation of its Nature and the Effects of Social Cognition', *Early Child Development and Care*, Vol. 87, pp. 47-57.

Slee, P. (1995), 'Peer Victimization and its Relationship to Depression Among Australian Primary School Students', *Personal Individual Differences*, Vol. 18, pp. 57-62.

Smart, B. (1993), *Postmodernism*, Routledge, London.

Smart, B. (1995), *Michel Foucault*, Routledge, London.

Smart, C. (1976), *Women, Crime and Criminology*, Routledge and Kegan Paul, London.

Smart, C. (1995), *Law, Crime and Sexuality*, Sage, London.

Smith, P. and Sharp, S. (1994), *School Bullying. Insights and Perspectives*, Routledge, London.

Snell, J., Rosenwald, R. and Robey, A. (1964), 'The Wife Beater's Wife: A Study of Family Interaction', *Archives of General Psychiatry*, Vol. 11, pp. 107-113.

Spaid, E. (1993), 'Justice: Young Activist Defends Abused Women', *The Christian Science Monitor*, Vol. 85, pp. 12-13.

Spelman, E. (1988), *Inessential Woman*, The Women's Press, London.

Spender, D. (1982), *Invisible Women*, The Women's Press, London.

Sousa, C. (1991), 'The Dating Violence Intervention Project', in B. Levy (ed.), *Dating Violence. Young Women in Danger*, The Seal Press, Seattle.

Stanley, L. (1990), *Feminist Praxis*, Routledge, London.

Stanley, L. and Wise, S. (1993), *Breaking Out Again: Feminist Ontology and Epistemology*, Routledge, London.

Statistics Canada (1995), *Canadian Crime Statistics 1994*, Canadian Centre for Justice Statistics, Ottawa.

Statistics New Zealand (1996), *New Zealand Now Crime*, Statistics New Zealand, Wellington.

Steffenmeier, D. (1980), 'Sex Differences in Patterns of Adult Crime, 1965-1977', *Social Forces*, Vol. 58, pp. 1080-1109.

Steinmetz, S. (1977), 'The Battered Husband Syndrome', *Victimology*, Vol. 2, pp. 499-509.

Stets, I. and Henderson, D. (1991), 'Contextual Factors Surrounding Conflict Resolution While Dating: Results From a National Study', *Family Relations*, Vol. 40, pp. 29-36.

Stets, I. and Pirog-Good, M. (1987), 'Violence in Dating Relationships', *Social Psychology Quarterly*, Vol. 50, pp. 237-246.

Straus, M. (1973), 'A General Systems Theory Approach to a Theory of Violence Between Family Members', *Social Science Information*, Vol. 12, pp. 105-125.

Strossen, N. (1995), *Defending Pornography. Free Speech, Sex, and the Fight for Women's Rights*, Abacus Books, London.

Stubbs, I. and Tolmie, I. (1994), 'Battered Woman Syndrome in Australia: A Challenge to Gender Bias in the Law?' in I. Stubbs (ed.), *Women, Male Violence and the Law*, Institute of Criminology Monograph Series No. 6, Sydney.

Sydie, R. (1987), *Natural Women, Cultured Men*, Open University, Milton Keynes.

Taylor, I. and Chandler, T. (1995), *Lesbians Talk Violent Relationships*, Scarlet Press, London.

Terry, R. (1970), 'Discrimination in the Handling of Juvenile Offenders', in P. Garabedian and D. Gibbons (eds), *Becoming Delinquent*, Aldine Press, Chicago.

Thomas, W. (1907), *Sex and Society*, Little Brown, Boston.

Thomas, W. (1967), *The Unadjusted Girl*, Harper and Row, New York.

Thorne, B. (1993), *Gender Play. Girls and Boys in School*, Rutgers University Press, New Brunswick.

Tiefer, L. (1987), 'In Pursuit of the Perfect Penis: The Medicalization of Male Sexuality' in M. Kimmel (ed.), *Changing Men: New Directions in Research on Men and Masculinity*, Sage, Newbury Park.

Toner, D. (1977), *The Facts of Rape*, Hutchinson, London.

Truscott, D. (1992), 'Intergenerational Transmission of Violent Behavior in Adolescent Males', *Aggressive Behavior*, Vol. 18, pp. 327-335.

Walker, L. (1984), *The Battered Woman Syndrome*, Springer Publishing, New York.

Walzer, M. (1987), *Interpretation and Social Criticism*, Harvard University Press, London.

Wattleton, F. (1989), 'The Case For National Action', *The Nation*, July 24-31, pp. 138-141.

Weber, M. (1985), *The Protestant Ethic and the Spirit of Capitalism*, Routledge, New York.

Weeks, J. (1986), *Sexuality*, Routledge, London.

Weeks, J. (1996), 'The Construction of Homosexuality', in S. Seidman (ed.), *Queer Theory/Sociology*, Blackwell, London.

Weeks, J. (1996), *Invented Moralities*, Columbia University Press, New York.

Weisberg, D. (1996), *Applications of Feminist Legal Theory to Women's Lives. Sex, Violence, Work, and Reproduction*, Temple University Press, Philadelphia.

Wenzel, L. (1993), 'About Battering', *New Directions for Women*, Vol. 22, pp. 8.

West, D., Roy, C. and Nichols, F. (1978), *Understanding Sexual Attack*, Heinemann Educational Books, London.

Wetherell, M. (1998), 'Positioning and Interpretive Repertoires: Conversation Analysis and Post-structuralism in Dialogue', *Discourse and Society*, Vol. 9, pp. 431-456.

Wetherell, M. and Maybin, J. (1996), 'The Distributed Self', in R. Stevens (ed.), *Understanding the Self*, Sage, London.

White, J. and Kowalski, R. (1994), 'Deconstructing the Myth of the Nonaggressive Woman: A Feminist Analysis', *Psychology of Women's Quarterley*, Vol.18, pp. 487-508.

Wilczynski, A. (1995), 'Child-killing By Parents: Social, Legal and Gender Issues', in R.E. Dobash, R. Dobash and L. Noaks (eds), *Gender and Crime*, University of Wales Press, Cardiff.

Williams, B. (1991), *Making Sense of Humanity and Other Philosophical Papers*, Cambridge University Press, Cambridge.

Williams, P. (1995), 'Meditations on Masculinity', in M. Berger, B. Wallis and S. Watson (eds.), *Constructing Masculinity*, Routledge, New York.

Willis, P. (1977), *Learning To Labor*, Columbia University Press, New York.

Wilson, E. (1975), *Sociobiology: The New Synthesis*, Harvard University Press, Cambridge.

Witkin, H. et al. (1983), 'Criminality in XYY and XXV Men', *Science*, pp. 547-555.

Yeatman, A. (1990), 'A Feminist Theory of Social Differentiation', in L. Nicholson (ed.), *Feminism/Postmodernism*, Routledge, New York.

Yllö, K. (1993), 'Through a Feminist Lens: Gender, Power and Violence', in R. Gelles and D. Loseke (eds), *Current Controversies on Family Violence*, Sage, London.

Yllö, K. and Bograd, M. (1988), *Feminist Perspectives on Wife Abuse*, Sage, London.

Young, I. (1990), 'The Ideal of Community and the Politics of Difference', in L. Nicholson (ed.), *Feminism/Postmodernism*, Routledge, London.

# Index